How To

D0130295

IMI *informati~*
S~ *~f~*

Financing a New Business

How to get the money to start your own business

PHIL STONE

How To Books

Published by How To Books Ltd,
3 Newtec Place, Magdalen Road,
Oxford OX4 1RE. United Kingdom.
Tel: (01865) 793806. Fax: (01865) 248780.
email: info@howtobooks.co.uk
www.howtobooks.co.uk

First edition 2001

British Library Cataloguing in Publication Data
A catalogue record for this book is available from
the British Library

Edited by Diana Brueton
Cover design by Shireen Nathoo Design
Cover image PhotoDisc

Produced for How To Books by Deer Park Productions
Typeset by PDQ Typesetting, Newcastle-under-Lyme, Staffs.
Printed and bound by Cromwell Press, Trowbridge, Wiltshire

NOTE: The material contained in this book is set out in good
faith for general guidance and no liability can be accepted
for loss or expense incurred as a result of relying in particular
circumstances on statements made in the book. Laws and
regulations are complex and liable to change, and readers should
check the current position with the relevant authorities before
making personal arrangements.

Contents

List of Illustrations

Preface

Raising finance for your business should not be difficult, providing you either have an existing profitable business or you have an idea for a new business that is feasible. Both of these aspects are important. If a lender is to finance your business they must be sure that you can meet the repayments. They are in business to lend money and make a profit.

Raising the right type of finance for your business is also important. There is little point in borrowing money on a short-term basis if you can only repay it over the long-term. This is a common mistake that small businesses make. They utilise short-term finance, for example a bank overdraft, to finance long-term expenditure such as the purchase of a new vehicle. This then leads to a reduction in short-term finance for working capital which could, in some circumstances, lead to business failure. You must match the type of finance to the type of expenditure.

You also need to be aware that in many cases you only get one chance to present your financing proposals to a lender. You therefore need to get it right first time. If the lender has doubts about your proposition it is unlikely that you will be given an opportunity to change it and present it again. You should have recognised the potential pitfalls in the first place and made provision for them in your plans. Once they have declined your request for funding you are unlikely to be able to persuade them to change their mind. Lenders are there to take a risk but that risk must be acceptable.

This book is designed to help you with all these problems. It covers the research you need to do to put your proposal together and outlines the way in which a potential source of finance will appraise your proposition. It shows you how to make the best use of your bank, and helps you to understand the implications of giving personal security for any debt. A number of different financing options are covered from the use of hire purchase and leasing through to the investments made by venture capitalists and business angels.

Finally you should always remember that a lender is there to assist you. If you are having problems at any time it is better to discuss them to try resolve the situation. Once you lose control of your finances you have lost control of your business. Lose control of your business and you will probably fail. This book will help you to stay in control of your finances and cope with any problems that may occur.

Phil Stone
phil@pkstone.demon.co.uk

1

Putting Your Proposal Together

Putting your proposal together is the most important aspect if you are to successfully raise finance for your business. Without a clear, feasible, realistic proposal you will not gain support. Provided you get this aspect right, you will have little difficulty in gaining finance. Lenders are there to lend money and are always looking for businesses to support.

Taking your time at this stage will reap rewards later on. Do not be in a hurry to try to gain finance before you have fine-tuned your proposal. Once the proposal has been seen and rejected by a potential funder it is difficult to go back and try again. As with all aspects of your business you need to get your proposal right first time.

Make sure that you thoroughly research the potential market for your business and cover all possible scenarios within your proposal. If there is a potential downside to your proposal then ensure that you have worked out your contingency plans. Lenders know that there is always a risk in running a business – no one can be 100% sure of success. Provided you take steps to minimise any risks lenders should be willing to provide funds. All lending carries a risk but that risk needs to be acceptable.

One final piece of advice before you even commence your proposal. Always be truthful. If you damage your integrity by not being completely open and honest within your proposal you will more than likely fail in your search for finance. Even if you do manage to gain the finance, once your fabrication has been discovered you will damage your reputation beyond repair. Once the finance has been repaid you are unlikely to gain further support from the same source.

RESEARCHING THE MARKET

The first task to undertake in putting your proposal together is to

11

thoroughly research the target market. Unless you understand what is happening in that market, and the trends and desires of the consumer, your business is not likely to succeed. You must be able to satisfy the demands of the consumer if you are to stay in business.

Before you even start to put your funding proposal together you will need to compile a full **marketing plan**. Ideally your funding proposal should be contained in a **business plan** which will explain all aspects of your business. Within this business plan you should summarise the market research that you have undertaken and outline your marketing strategies for the future. For full details of how you compile a marketing plan and a business plan have a look at *The Ultimate Business Plan* and *Make Marketing Work for You*. (See Further Reading at the end of this book.)

Establishing the market and potential customers

Without customers you will not survive. Unless you can establish who your customers are, how much they will pay, and where they will buy from, you cannot formulate a successful marketing strategy.

There are six questions that you need to answer:

- Who are your potential customers?
- What do they buy?
- Why do they buy the products that they buy?
- How much influence do others have on the purchase decision?
- When do they buy?
- Where do they buy?

Who are your potential customers?
Customers could come from either a narrow or a broad segment of the total population. They can be divided into a wide variety of headings, for example:

- age bands
- occupations
- standard of education
- income levels
- family position, e.g. married, single and with or without children
- location.

The list is virtually endless. However, it is important that you segment your potential customers correctly.

What do they buy?

You need to understand which products consumers purchase. Conversely, you need to establish what products consumers will not buy. In order to gain this information you will probably need to undertake some form of consumer survey.

Why do they buy the products that they buy?

Most products in the market are available in different forms. As an example, consider toiletry products such as soap and toothpaste. You must therefore establish exactly what it is that influences consumer choice. In many cases it could be brand image or customer loyalty.

How much influence do others have on the purchase decision?

A prime example is the market for children's clothing and footwear. It sometimes makes no difference whatsoever what the parents think, the children will influence the buying decision through their desire to be trendy. They have to keep pace with the latest fashions and have the same as their peers.

When do they buy?

In some markets there are obvious seasonal trends, for example, Christmas cards and wrapping paper. Gardening products are also more likely to be purchased from perhaps March to September. Many purchases follow a similar pattern although others can be more difficult to track.

In general though, for items that are purchased frequently, for example food, it can be difficult to establish any trend. Some people may shop only once a week and purchase sufficient for that week. Others, however, may visit the shop on a daily basis as part of their routine on the way home from work.

Where do they buy?

With the availability of many different sources of goods, especially with the introduction of shopping on the Internet, this question will be of extreme importance to you. You may have the best product in the world, but unless you are in the right place, at the right time, your opportunities will be limited.

Using a SWOT analysis

SWOT is the acronym for strengths, weaknesses, opportunities and threats. A SWOT analysis will make you think about the positive

Strengths	Weaknesses
Something that you are doing right or are good at. It may be a skill, a competence or a competitive advantage that you have over rivals. Questions to ask yourself: • What are your advantages? • What do you do well?	Something that you lack or do poorly when compared to rivals. A condition that puts you at a disadvantage. Questions to ask yourself: • What could be improved? • What is done badly? • What should be avoided?
Opportunities	**Threats**
A realistic avenue for future growth in the business. Something to be used to develop a competitive advantage. Questions to ask yourself: • What are the trends in the market? • How can they be exploited? • What chances are there for me?	A factor that you may or may not have control over that could lead to a decline in business. Questions to ask yourself: • What obstacles do you face? • What is your competition doing? • What effect is increasing technology having?

Fig. 1. SWOT analysis grid.

aspects of your existing or proposed business as well as the negative ones.

The analysis is usually undertaken by using a grid to consider how you will match the strengths to the opportunities and how you will overcome the weaknesses and threats (see Figure 1).

Conducting a SWOT analysis is, in effect, the construction of a non-financial balance sheet. Existing or potential assets are in the left columns represented by the strengths and opportunities, and existing or potential liabilities are in the right columns represented by the weaknesses and threats.

The key points to remember when using a SWOT analysis are:

• build on strengths
• resolve weaknesses
• exploit opportunities
• avoid threats.

Assessing the competition

Understanding your competitors is crucial if you are to obtain a competitive advantage. It is only in this way that you can exploit the opportunities available to you and counter the prospective threats.

Competition will come in four different ways:

- direct
- indirect
- industry
- linked.

It is extremely important for you to have as much information on your competitors as possible. If you do not know what your competitors are doing there is little prospect of you being able to compete. Ideally you will need to assess your competitors under the following broad headings:

- Exactly who they are.
- What their marketing objectives relate to.
- What sort of marketing strategies they employ.
- Whether they have any strengths and weaknesses.

Once you have gained as much information as possible you can use a SWOT analysis to put it into a defined, logical format.

Having a clear competitive advantage

Competitive advantage is critical to your marketing. You must offer some form of differentiation from other businesses in the same market if you are to persuade consumers to buy from you. Competitive advantage can take two main forms, either of which may or may not be readily visible in the market:

- Financial – either through efficiency savings which lead to lower costs of production and/or a lower selling price to the consumer.

- Differentiation in service – perhaps through longer opening hours, an improved delivery service, a measurable difference in the quality of service or a higher quality product.

There is, of course, a further alternative which would combine both of the above forms. However, there is a danger that trying to be competitive on all fronts could result in a mixed message being sent to consumers. You must remember that consumers do not always buy on price alone. Sometimes quality is more important. It is therefore not always appropriate to try to combine high quality with low price. Consumer expectation also plays a part in the formula.

Compiling your marketing strategy

Your marketing strategy will focus on the key areas of:

- products
- price
- place
- promotion.

In order for your business to succeed you must have:

- the right products
- at the right price
- in the right place
- and at the right time.

In addition your customers must be aware of your business. You can have the greatest product in the world but unless consumers are aware of it they cannot possibly buy it.

When you actually write your marketing strategy, you will bring together all these components into a logical framework. You must understand that marketing is the backbone of your business. You may be able to raise vast sums of finance but unless your marketing strategy succeeds you might be unable to repay that finance.

COMPILING THE FORECASTS

Forecasts are the next essential component of your funding proposal. They will be used to show the anticipated flow of cash through the business, the profits or indeed losses that will be made, and finally the financial strength of the business in terms of assets and liabilities.

Cash flow forecast

A **cash flow forecast** is used to forecast the cash that will flow into and out of your business (see Figure 2). It is not concerned with anything other than cash and will therefore not indicate whether you

	Sep 01 £	Oct 01 £	Nov 01 £	Dec 01 £	Jan 02 £	Feb 02 £	Mar 02 £	Apr 02 £	May 02 £	Jun 02 £	Jul 02 £	Aug 02 £	Total £
Receipts													
Invoiced sales	69,769	69,769	69,769	69,769	37,457	37,457	69,769	221,932	13,957	69,769	96,794	96,794	923,005
	69,769	69,769	69,769	69,769	37,457	37,457	69,769	221,932	13,957	69,769	96,794	96,794	923,005
Payments													
Invoiced costs	18,425	22,612	29,575	22,905	22,906	29,574	22,906	22,905	29,574	22,906	22,905	29,575	296,768
Directors' remuneration	4,666	4,666	4,666	4,666	4,666	4,666	4,666	4,666	4,666	4,666	4,666	4,666	55,992
Wages and salaries	15,916	15,916	15,916	18,833	18,833	21,333	21,333	21,333	21,333	21,333	21,333	21,333	234,745
Overdraft interest	924	794	712	560	590	796	816	255	1	2	–	–	5,450
PAYE/NI	2,210	2,470	2,470	2,470	2,820	2,820	3,120	3,119	3,120	3,120	3,119	3,120	33,978
VAT	–	19,869	–	–	15,450	–	–	38,113	–	–	15,975	–	89,407
	42,141	66,327	53,339	49,434	65,265	59,189	52,841	90,391	58,694	52,027	67,998	58,694	716,340
Net cash flow	27,628	3,442	16,430	20,335	(27,808)	(21,732)	16,298	131,541	(44,737)	17,742	28,796	38,100	206,665
Opening bank	(125,075)	(97,447)	(94,005)	(77,575)	(57,240)	(85,048)	(106,780)	(89,852)	41,689	(3,048)	14,694	43,490	(125,075)
Closing bank	(97,447)	(94,005)	(77,575)	(57,240)	(85,048)	(106,780)	(89,852)	41,689	(3,048)	14,694	43,490	81,590	81,590

Fig. 2. Cash flow forecast.

are making profits or losses. It is a vital tool in controlling your business to ensure that liquidity is maintained.

Liquidity, in terms of actual cash, is essential to all businesses no matter what their size. Orders from customers are of no value whatsoever if you do not have the funds to manufacture the goods. In the same way, a warehouse full of stock will not pay the wages unless those goods can be sold and thereby converted into cash.

Profit and loss
Profit and loss forecasts are also sometimes referred to as **operating budgets** (see Figure 3). In many ways these will take the same format as your cash flow forecasts although you must remember that you are dealing with profit and not cash. This will, for example, mean that the forecasted sales will be entered in the actual month that they are made and not when you anticipate receiving the cash.

One of the other important aspects to remember is that profit does not equate to cash. Because you are now entering profit in the month in which it is made it does not mean that you have actually made a profit. Profit is only received when the cash itself is received.

The final point that you need to remember when compiling profit and loss forecasts is that not all elements of the cash flow forecast will be included. You will only include items that are directly related to trading activity. As examples, you will not include within your business income items such as:

- capital introduced
- loans received.

Likewise, on the expenditure side you will not include such items as:

- funds used for the purchase of fixed assets.

Balance sheet
The final component of your forecasted accounts is the **balance sheet**. All too often, however, it is totally ignored. This is a fundamental mistake because you can only identify the individual components of working capital by preparing a forecasted balance sheet.

Without such a forecast you cannot identify the following:

- stock levels held
- debtors outstanding
- creditors outstanding.

Fig. 3. Profit and loss forecast table.

	Sep 01 £	Oct 01 £	Nov 01 £	Dec 01 £	Jan 02 £	Feb 02 £	Mar 02 £	Apr 02 £	May 02 £	Jun 02 £	Jul 02 £	Aug 02 £	Total £
Turnover													
Product sales	47,500	47,500	47,500	20,000	20,000	47,500	177,00	–	47,500	70,500	70,500	70,500	666,000
IT sales	11,878	11,878	11,878	11,878	11,878	11,878	11,878	11,878	11,878	11,878	11,878	11,878	142,536
	59,378	59,378	59,378	31,878	31,878	59,378	188,878	11,878	59,378	82,378	82,378	82,378	808,536
Direct costs													
Purchases	7,601	7,602	7,602	7,602	7,602	7,602	7,602	7,602	7,602	7,602	7,602	7,602	91,223
Sub-contract	641	642	641	642	641	642	641	641	642	641	642	641	7,697
	8,242	8,244	8,243	8,244	8,243	8,244	8,243	8,243	8,244	8,243	8,244	8,243	98,920
Gross profit	51,136	51,134	51,135	23,634	23,635	51,134	180,635	3,635	51,134	74,135	74,134	74,135	709,616
Overheads													
Directors' remuneration	5,226	5,226	5,226	5,226	5,226	5,226	5,225	5,226	5,226	5,226	5,226	5,226	62,711
Wages and salaries	17,826	17,826	17,826	21,093	21,093	23,893	23,893	23,893	23,893	23,892	23,893	23,893	262,914
Rent	1,085	1,085	1,085	1,085	1,085	1,085	1,085	1,085	1,085	1,085	1,085	1,085	13,020
Training	–	3,054	–	–	3,054	–	–	3,054	–	–	3,054	–	12,216
Telephone	1,027	1,027	1,027	1,027	1,027	1,027	1,027	1,027	1,027	1,027	1,027	1,027	12,324
Printing and stationery	469	469	469	469	469	469	469	469	469	469	469	469	5,628
Postage and packaging	159	159	159	159	159	159	159	159	159	159	159	159	1,908
Equipment rental	637	637	637	637	637	637	637	637	637	637	637	637	7,644
Insurance	673	673	673	673	673	673	673	673	673	673	673	673	8,076
Motor expenses	2,260	2,260	2,260	2,260	2,260	2,260	2,260	2,260	2,260	2,260	2,260	2,260	27,120
Travel and subsistence	1,356	1,356	1,356	1,356	1,356	1,356	1,356	1,356	1,356	1,356	1,356	1,356	16,272
Advertising	3,164	3,413	3,413	3,413	3,413	3,413	3,413	3,413	3,413	3,413	3,413	3,413	40,707
Entertainment	212	212	212	212	212	212	212	212	212	212	212	212	2,544
Legal and professional	307	307	307	307	307	307	307	307	307	307	307	307	3,684
General expenses	812	812	812	812	812	812	812	812	812	812	812	812	9,744
Depreciation	94	94	93	94	94	94	93	94	94	94	93	94	1,125
	35,307	38,610	35,555	38,823	41,877	41,623	41,621	44,047	41,623	41,622	44,676	41,623	487,637
Operating profit	15,829	12,524	15,580	(15,189)	(18,242)	9,511	139,014	(41,042)	9,511	32,513	29,458	32,512	221,979
Interest expense													
Overdraft interest	924	794	712	560	590	796	816	255	1	2	–	–	5,450
	924	794	712	560	590	796	816	255	1	2	–	–	5,450
Net profit	14,905	11,730	14,868	(15,749)	(18,832)	8,715	138,198	(41,297)	9,510	32,511	29,458	32,512	216,529
Cumulative	14,905	26,635	41,503	25,754	6,922	15,637	153,835	112,538	122,048	154,559	184,017	216,529	216,529

Fig. 3. Profit and loss forecast.

19

Without such information you could find that you are running your business without sufficient liquidity. For example, you may be holding too much stock which in turn means that you are using cash unnecessarily. By the same token, you may have insufficient money due from debtors to meet your ongoing liability to your creditors. Either of these situations could be distorting your cash flow forecast. Once again, therefore, you need to be looking at the balance sheet forecasts in conjunction with your cash flow, and profit and loss forecasts.

Break-even point

Break-even point is something that is totally ignored by most businesses. In simple terms it is the sales that need to be made to cover all of the business's costs over a defined period (see Figure 4). Before you can calculate your break-even point you need to establish your gross profit margin. This is the amount of money left after taking the sales figure and deducting the cost of those sales, normally referred to as variable costs. Once you have established this margin you then know how much money you have left to pay the overheads, or fixed costs of the business.

The break-even point is then calculated by dividing your fixed costs by the gross margin and then multiplying by 100. As a specific example, assume that you have fixed costs of £20,000 per annum and your gross margin is 40%. This would mean that your break-even point equates to:

$$\frac{£20,000}{40} \times 100 = £50,000$$

In simple terms this means that just to break even, i.e. not make a profit or loss, you would need to have sales of £50,000 per annum in order to cover all your variable and fixed costs.

WORKING OUT HOW MUCH YOU NEED

Once you have completed your forecasts you should be in a position to work out how much finance you need. At this stage it is not necessary to consider where it will come from. Apart from your own contribution the source of funding will depend on what it is required for. This aspect is considered in Chapter 2 but for the moment you just need to establish the total funding.

Gross margin percentage

Monthly fixed costs	50%	45%	40%	35%	30%	25%	20%	15%
£5,000	£10,000	£11,100	£12,500	£14,300	£16,700	£20,000	£25,000	£33,300
£4,500	£9,000	£10,000	£11,300	£12,900	£15,000	£18,000	£22,500	£30,000
£4,000	£8,000	£8,900	£10,000	£11,400	£13,300	£16,000	£20,000	£26,700
£3,500	£7,000	£7,800	£8,800	£10,000	£11,700	£14,000	£17,500	£23,300
£3,000	£6,000	£6,700	£7,500	£8,600	£10,000	£12,000	£15,000	£20,000
£2,500	£5,000	£5,600	£6,300	£7,100	£8,300	£10,000	£12,500	£16,700
£2,000	£4,000	£4,400	£5,000	£5,700	£6,700	£8,000	£10,000	£13,300
£1,500	£3,000	£3,300	£3,800	£4,300	£5,000	£6,000	£7,500	£10,000
£1,000	£2,000	£2,200	£2,500	£2,900	£3,300	£4,000	£5,000	£6,700

Fig. 4. Break-even sales calculator.

Example
With fixed costs of £4,500 per month and a gross margin of 35%, sales of £12,900 per month are required to break even. If the gross margin drops to 30% then sales of £15,000 per month are required to break even. Note that the decrease in gross margin of just 5% requires an increase in sales of 16% to retain break-even.

Being realistic

This is a crucial aspect of your proposal. You must be entirely realistic in the amount of funding that you require. Remember, your proposal must be viable and the risk must be acceptable to the potential funder. It is not too late at this stage to revise your forecasts, especially if the debt finance required is out of proportion to your own contribution.

When you compiled your forecasts you probably included every single item of expenditure that you considered necessary. Perhaps some expenditure on equipment which would be 'nice to have' can be deferred until a later stage. This decision can only be taken by you. If you consider that the funding required is absolutely necessary it will be up to you to justify your decision.

Gearing

Gearing is the relationship between your funds in the business, the owner's capital, and borrowed money or debt. Let us assume that your business has £5,000 capital and you are seeking £7,500 of borrowed funds. Gearing is calculated by dividing one by the other and can be expressed in one of two ways:

- gearing percentage – £7,500 ÷ £5,000 × 100 = 150%
- gearing ratio – £7,500 ÷ £5,000 = 1.5:1

This shows that for every £1 of capital there are debts of £1.50. Gearing of more than 100% or 1:1 is considered high. Gearing of less than 100% or 1:1 is considered low. This means that with low gearing the owner is shouldering the majority of the risk. Conversely, with high gearing the lender is assuming more risk than the owner.

For a small business looking to raise finance, the lender will probably be looking for gearing as close to 100% as possible. Having said that, there is no 'perfect' gearing ratio and each proposition is considered on its merits.

Holding funds in reserve

Many entrepreneurs make the mistake of investing all their available financial resources into their own business instead of obtaining a balanced mix of funding. In some cases there appears to be an aversion to obtaining debt finance. This can be a costly mistake if, for example, you invest all your cash into your business and your finances do not go as planned. It can be difficult to raise debt finance to put matters back on an even keel.

It is far better to obtain a balance from the outset and have your own funds in reserve should things go wrong. Say, for example, you estimate that you need £10,000 for your business and you actually hold that in cash yourself. It is preferable to invest £5,000 of your own money and obtain the balance by debt finance. On a gearing basis this would not be an unattractive proposition to a lender and it does, of course, leave you with cash to spare, possibly to invest in the future.

WRITING THE BUSINESS PLAN

Your business plan is your one and only chance to impress a potential lender and you should, therefore, take your time and not be in a rush to complete it. The business plan needs to detail every aspect of your business, explaining your plans for the future and exactly why you need finance. It will also need to show quite clearly how that finance is to be repaid.

Covering all the angles

The ideal business plan will be so thorough that the potential lender will have few, if any, questions on your proposal. You need to cover all eventualities and make adequate provision for any unforeseen circumstances. It is, for example, acceptable to allow for some slippage in the receipt of debtor monies. Provided you can explain why you have built in such a contingency and that it is realistic it will not be criticised by the potential lender.

The lender needs to ensure that you have considered all possible angles so that, if things do go wrong, at least you have a strategy in place to deal with them.

Using fact not fiction

Throughout the course of doing your research you will have discovered numerous facts and figures. You will no doubt have also unearthed the opinions and assertions of many people either connected or unconnected with your market. The important job that you now face is to sort out the fact from the fiction.

Within your business plan you will make a number of assumptions, not just related to the financial forecasts, and it is important that you back up these assumptions with supporting facts. The target audience for your business plan will need to be convinced that what you are telling them is true and the only way that you can do this is by presenting them with firm evidence.

At all costs avoid waffle and unsubstantiated claims. If you are going to make a claim then back it up with hard facts and evidence. For example, 'the market has increased from £Xm to £Ym over the last two years, and, according to research carried out by Anytown University, growth will continue at a rate of Z% per annum for the foreseeable future.'

This demonstrates to your target audience that you have done your research, understood the results and converted this information into an opportunity for your business. Remember, if the target audience is sufficiently interested in your business plan they may well do some research of their own in order to substantiate your claims. You need to make sure that the facts they obtain will match your own.

Answer all the potential questions

It cannot be emphasised enough, *your business plan needs to answer all the questions of your potential funder*. It should be presented in an easy-to-read and logical format in order to persuade your target audience that you do know what you are talking about.

The trick here is to put yourself in the position of the potential funder. You know the sort of questions you have already asked yourself when doing your research and you need to ensure that the business plan answers all these.

A potential funder will not be impressed if they have a question that you are unable to answer. All this demonstrates to them is that your research is inadequate and, based on this fact alone, they may simply decline your proposition. As previously said, you may only get one chance, so get it right first time.

Making sure words and figures match

One final point on writing your business plan. You will, of course, include the financial forecasts that have probably been prepared by your accountant and reference to these will be made within the body of the business plan. Check and double-check that both the words and the figures match. For example, if the business plan states that growth in profitability of X% in the first year will be achieved, make sure that your forecasts actually show this growth.

Any silly mistakes between the words and figures within the business plan will only cast doubt on your proposal. It would be a shame to have spent so much time putting your proposal together to fail on something so simple. Before submitting your proposal it would also be wise to get a third party to check the content for you. All too often you will see what you *want* to read rather than what is actually written. Once your proposal has been submitted it is too late to change it.

KEY POINTS

- Your funding proposal is the key to raising finance – take your time and get it absolutely right before you submit it to a potential funder.

- Make sure that you have thoroughly researched the market and formulated a full marketing plan.

- Use a SWOT analysis to identify the positive aspects of your business which can be exploited and the negative aspects which need to be countered.

- When you compile your financial forecasts you must ensure that they are accurate as well as realistic in terms of the amount of funding that you need.

- If possible avoid investing all your own money into your business – it is better to hold funds in reserve and obtain debt finance on a matching basis.

- When you write your funding proposal or business plan make sure that you cover all possible angles and have contingency plans to cover unforeseen circumstances.

- Before you submit your funding proposal check it through thoroughly for any mistakes – you only have one chance, get it right first time.

2

Looking for the Right Type of Finance

Having completed your funding proposal it is now time to consider where you are going to try to gain the finance. Having the right type of finance for your business is just as important as gaining finance in the first place. Having the wrong type of finance could have severe implications in the future. For example, buying a major asset to be used in the long-term by raising short-term finance is going to lead to repayment problems unless you have the means to repay that funding in the short-term. You also need to have the right balance of funding, often referred to as the financial package. Requesting the wrong type of finance, or not having the right balance of funding, could lead to your proposition being declined. This chapter will help to lead you through the process of choosing the right type of finance by explaining in brief the various forms of finance and their uses.

PUTTING YOUR MONEY IN FIRST

Before you can even consider raising funds from external sources you must make your own investment. This investment takes two main forms:

- financial
- non-financial.

Financial investment, as the name suggests, is a direct injection of cash into your business. If you are operating as a limited liability company, this could take the form of share capital or director's loan. If you operate either as a sole trader or partnership, it will be classified as owner's or partner's capital.

The decision as to which type of business to operate can be complex. There are advantages and disadvantages to operating as a sole trader, or as a partnership, or as a limited liability company.

From the outset you need to seek professional advice on this aspect.

Non-financial investment is the introduction of assets that you may already own, for example motor vehicles, tools and equipment. These need to be carefully valued for inclusion in your financial records. If you are introducing assets into your business in this way you are advised to seek the help of an accountant. This will ensure that your assets are correctly valued and that they comply with any Inland Revenue guidelines.

Showing commitment

There are no hard-and-fast rules about how much of your own money you must invest in your business before you can gain finance. One of the important factors that the potential lender will be looking for is that you are showing a total commitment to your business. The simple fact is that if you personally are not prepared to risk sufficient funds the lender is unlikely to either.

This relates back to the question of gearing that was explained in Chapter 1. It will also to a certain extent depend on the type of finance that you require. For short-term finance, for example a bank overdraft, it is likely that gearing of 100% – i.e. matching finance – will be possible. On the other hand long-term lending may only require a small contribution from you, for example the purchase of a vehicle may only require a 10% deposit from you, equating to a gearing ratio of 1,000%.

Borrowing your own contribution

It might seem a little strange that I should suggest that you can borrow your own contribution to invest in your business. This is, however, a source of finance that is often overlooked by business owners. It does, however, need to be approached with caution. You still need to find the funds to repay the debt and in all probability the source of that repayment will come from your own drawings from the business.

The main asset that many people will own is their house. Even if you have an existing mortgage, provided you have sufficient equity it may be possible to borrow money against the security of your house. Some home loan providers will not consider loans to invest in businesses yet others will. With the level of competition that there is in the mortgage market it may pay you to shop around.

A further factor that you need to consider is the possibility that you may have other assets that you can sell to raise finance. For example, as children many people collect items of possibly marginal value at the time which in later years languish in a loft. Postage stamps would be a good example. It may be that 30 or 40 years on those stamps will have some value. Perhaps very little, but possibly quite a lot. The point is they are no good to you where they are now. Examine what is important and what could be changed. This may open up additional ways and means to provide finance for your business from your own resources.

Gaining the support of your family

Running your own business can have a dramatic effect on your family life and it is important that you have the support of your family from the outset. If you have previously been in employment you can, for example, say goodbye to the standard 9-to-5 working life. You may find that your home life and your business life suddenly become intertwined.

You must also remember that if you are giving up a job to start your own business, the regular salary or wage payments will also cease. Your income will depend entirely on how successful your business becomes. This emphasises the need to have proper funding in place from the start. It also underlines the advice given in the previous chapter of having something in reserve.

Working for yourself is not an easy option and it will require hard work with the probability of long hours. Remember that paid holidays and days off sick will be a thing of the past. Weekends will also probably be encroached upon to enable you to deal with basic administration.

Unless you have support from your family you will be fighting to survive on two separate fronts, at home and at work. You cannot afford these distractions. You must be able to concentrate your efforts on running your business.

USING SHORT-TERM FINANCE

Obviously **short-term finance** is designed to be used and repaid in the short-term. In terms of a business this is often referred to as **working capital finance**. It is used to finance working capital and pay creditors and is then itself repaid following receipt of funds from debtors. The most common form of short-term finance is provided by banks in the form of an overdraft.

Overdrafts

Whilst an **overdraft** may be the most common form of short-term finance it is also probably the most abused. It is often used for purchasing assets for which long-term finance should have been obtained. An overdraft is a revolving form of credit up to an agreed limit. This limit is agreed in advance and is then available for use, usually for a defined period normally ranging from a few months up to one year. You are then free to draw on that facility as and when required.

Overdrafts do not have any defined repayment, although the bank will normally insist when granting the facility that it is repayable in full on demand. This does, of course, mean that it can be taken away just as quickly as it can be granted. Overdrafts are looked at in greater detail in Chapter 4.

Bridging loans

Bridging loans are usually granted by a bank to allow expenditure to be incurred pending receipt of the proceeds from the sale of an asset, usually a house or other form of property. At one time these were freely available although now their use is strictly controlled. Previously you may have been able to gain a bridging loan as soon as your property was placed on the market. It is now necessary to have at least exchanged contracts on the sale in order that the repayment period is clearly defined.

The reason for this is that the interest on the loan can soon mount up and such interest needs to be covered on a regular basis, typically monthly. The use of bridging loans for short-term finance has, therefore, declined in recent years although for the right purpose, and under the right circumstances, they are still available.

Factoring and invoice discounting

Both **factoring** and **invoice discounting** allow you to obtain finance against your outstanding debtors. This means that instead of waiting for your debtors to pay you, you sell the debt to the factor or invoice discounter and they pay you in advance an agreed percentage of the debt. They are then repaid when your debtor actually pays you.

In general these forms of finance are only available to established businesses. In addition there are minimum criteria relating to the annual sales turnover of the business and usually this form of funding is not appropriate for businesses turning over less than £250,000. Factoring or invoice discounting can be both complex and expensive. Both these forms of finance are looked at in greater detail in Chapter 7.

Trade credit

Obtaining **credit** from your suppliers is also another easy form of short-term finance. It can also be the cheapest form of finance. You are, effectively, using other people's money to finance your business although no interest or other charges are payable. The terms of such credit can vary widely from a few weeks up to many months and will depend, in many cases, upon the particular type of business that you operate.

It must be stressed, however, that you must not abuse your creditors. As with a bank overdraft, the facility can be just as easily withdrawn as it can be granted. Following legislation that is being phased in from 1998 you can also be penalised by your creditors if you do not pay them on time. They will be entitled to charge you interest at penal rates. This aspect is also explained in greater detail in Chapter 7.

USING LONG-TERM FINANCE

If you are considering purchasing any form of fixed asset, for example plant and machinery or vehicles, you must obtain long-term finance. In addition, it is prudent to obtain that finance on repayment terms linked to the likely life of the asset. As an example, if you are purchasing an asset with a working life of, say, three years, it would be prudent to repay the necessary finance over the same term. In most cases the lender will indeed insist upon this. It would be futile them lending you money over ten years for an asset that will only last for three years.

Loans

Business loans are available from a wide variety of sources, and indeed on a wide range of terms and conditions. Some are secured on assets of one kind or another and some are available on an unsecured basis. As with all forms of finance, you need to know and understand the exact conditions under which the loan is being made available.

One thing to look out for is early repayment penalties. Even if you do have the means to repay the loan early it could cost you extra in terms of a fee or penalty interest. Most loans are covered by Consumer Credit legislation with 'cooling off' periods, and a lot of somewhat dubious terms and conditions that were previously imposed have been made illegal.

The majority of business loans are provided by banks with interest usually calculated in one of two ways:

- fixed rate interest
- variable rate interest.

Bank loans are considered in detail in Chapter 4.

Hire purchase

Hire purchase is one of the most common forms of finance for individuals and it can be a very flexible form of finance for businesses. You only have to walk down your local high street to see the range of hire purchase schemes that are available, some more expensive than others.

Hire purchase is an agreement to buy an asset, for example a motor vehicle or computer equipment, with defined repayments over an agreed term. Depending upon the agreement, ownership of the asset may or may not pass to you immediately. Some agreements, for obvious reasons, do not allow ownership until all instalments have been paid.

Leasing

Leasing is an extremely flexible form of funding. A lease is negotiated with the lessor who acquires the asset that has been chosen by the lessee. The assets which can be leased are wide and varied. Photocopiers, computer systems, office furniture, motor vehicles, machine tools, and heavy plant and equipment are all examples.

Leasing should be distinguished from hiring. Hiring requires the user to select an item from stock already held by the hirer. Leasing enables the lessee to select any item from any manufacturer or supplier. The choice is therefore unlimited. The leasing agreement will be tailor-made for the actual asset involved.

There are three types of lease:

- finance lease
- operating lease
- contract hire.

Leasing and hire purchase, and the advantages and disadvantages of each, are looked at in Chapter 6.

Equity

Equity finance is gained by offering shares in your business. It is only available to businesses that are incorporated into a limited liability company. In very general terms it is offered by specialist lenders in one of the following two categories:

- venture capitalists
- business angels.

Venture capitalists are usually only interested in large funding proposals, typically being a minimum funding requirement of £250,000. However there are some venture capitalists which operate on a localised regional basis who will consider investments as low as £5,000.

Business angels, on the other hand, are individuals who will invest in a business, taking shares in exchange for that investment. In addition they will tend to take a personal interest in the business, perhaps offering their own expertise in the running of that business. Further details on equity investors is contained in Chapter 9.

USING DEVELOPMENT FINANCE

Development finance is a highly specialised area, in addition to which it is considered to be very high-risk funding. For that reason it can also be expensive as the risk is directly related to the reward, i.e. the costs of borrowing. It is similar to equity finance in that shares in the business are obtained in return for the investment.

Seed capital

Seed capital is a form of venture capital that is usually provided to allow a business concept to be developed. As the name would suggest it is finance that is designed to help a business to develop an original idea. Seed capital can be used in a variety of ways including:

- market research
- development of a prototype.

Seed capital can also be used to initiate the manufacturing of the product and subsequent promotion activities. There are a number of institutions that provide seed capital although many will only consider specific types of business. In addition, the maximum level of such finance varies between institutions. Some will only provide up to £50,000 and others will finance as much as £500,000 of the total costs.

Research and development finance

Research and development finance is similar to seed capital although it is generally only available to established businesses that are profitable or, at the very minimum, breaking even. It can be used for the development of new products or markets, or provide additional working capital to fund growth and expansion. It may also be used for the development of new manufacturing methods to either increase production or improve production efficiency.

As with seed capital it can be an expensive form of finance because of the high risk involved. Investment returns of in excess of 30% per annum are not unusual. Investors will usually also be looking for a repayment route within five to seven years.

Grants and awards

There is a wide variety of grants and awards available to businesses, although in some circumstances these will relate to your geographical location within the UK. In addition, they are normally linked to capital expenditure or job creation although there are some exceptions. The main providers of grants and awards are:

- Department of Trade and Industry
- Business Links
- local authorities.

In many cases the grant or award is only available as 'gap' finance. This means that if the funding can be raised from conventional sources, for example your bank, the grant may not be available. Another important fact is that normally no expenditure may be incurred before the grant application has been accepted and agreed. This is a vital point. Many businesses lose out on the grants and awards available purely because they do not abide by the rules. This aspect is so important that I have devoted the whole of Chapter 8 to the sort of support that could be available and how to go about making the most of the opportunities that may be there.

KEY POINTS

- It is extremely important that you gain the right type of finance – short-term finance for short-term requirements and long-term finance for long-term requirements.

- Your own investment in your business must be made first – no lender will consider finance without your own contribution.

- The commitment and support of your family is vital – running your own business is hard work with the probability of long hours and lost weekends.

- Always check on the availability of grants or awards before you incur any expenditure – you run the risk of missing out if you do not abide by the rules.

3

Understanding the Lender's Point of View

If you are going to raise finance successfully for your business it is important that you understand the lender's point of view. There is little point in making an application for finance if such application falls outside the lender's criteria. Before you submit your proposal to any funder it is worthwhile having an informal discussion about your plans which will, at least, give you an idea of whether or not the funder is likely to be interested.

This will save you a lot of time and trouble later when you actually come to submitting a full proposal. For obvious reasons you will not approach those funders that have shown no interest in funding your business. It will also give you an idea of the sort of criteria that the funder has for lending the money that you require. They will also give you guidance on the type of funding that will probably be most relevant to meet your circumstances.

SUBMITTING YOUR PROPOSAL

Having put together your full business plan and funding proposal, the way in which it is submitted to potential funders is extremely important. The proposal needs to be sufficiently attractive to generate interest. Remember, the funder is there to lend money but they will receive a large number of applications and, therefore, pressure on their time is intense.

Having had informal discussions with the potential funder, you will know exactly to whom to send your proposal. It should be sent together with a covering letter outlining the project in brief and the funding required. In many ways it will be in the same form as the synopsis contained in the business plan. Make sure that your covering letter is no longer than a single page. Potential funders do not want to read a long and rambling account of your plans that merely duplicates the business plan. What you have to do is grab their attention sufficiently to make them want to actually read the business plan.

Presentation is important

Just because you have submitted your proposal does not actually mean that it will be read in full. Unless it is well presented and written in an easy to read format it could be that the potential funder will start to read it, find it difficult to understand, and then merely decline to assist you on the basis that they have not got the time, or indeed the inclination, to study your proposal further.

I have no doubt that funders would refute this suggestion but I can assure you it does happen. I did it myself when working as a lending manager with a major high street bank. The extreme pressures on my time meant that unless I could quickly grasp the content of a proposal, and be sufficiently impressed with the proposed business, then a simple letter of decline would be sent.

Allowing sufficient time for analysis

Assuming that you have got over the first hurdle and actually generated some interest in the potential funder, you must allow them sufficient time to make a judgement as to whether to assist or not. If you pester them for a quick decision you will certainly get one but it will not be the decision you want.

Remember that it may have taken you many weeks to research and put together your business plan and if it is to receive proper consideration by a funder they will need time. You cannot expect to make an appointment to see them, take along your business plan and receive a decision on the spot.

I would not recommend that you contact the potential funder until at least seven days has passed following your initial submission. If the funder wants to discuss anything with you before that time has elapsed they will contact you. After the seven-day period you can then contact them to see whether they have had the time to look at your proposal and whether you can make an appointment to discuss it further. Even if they have not had time to look at your proposal they may still be willing for you to make an appointment, because with the pressure on their time this could in any event be for some seven to ten days hence.

BEING PREPARED FOR THE MEETING

Preparation for the meeting with your potential funder is critical. You do not want to fail purely because you have not prepared sufficiently. The first thing to do is to read, and then read again your business plan and funding proposal. You must know it inside out and be absolutely ready to answer any questions that the funder will raise. Be assured that they will prepare thoroughly for the meeting and will already have a set of questions for which they will require answers.

Remember that some time will have elapsed between the actual completion of your business plan and your meeting with the funder. If there have been any significant developments on your proposals make sure that you have details. In some cases you may be asking a number of different types of funders for money to support your proposals. If you have gained any agreement from another funder, make sure that you have copies of any correspondence available. Where you have a package of funding proposed from a number of different sources you may find that you can gain agreement in principle from one, conditional on the remaining funds being agreed.

Showing enthusiasm

You must have sincere enthusiasm for your proposal if you are to generate enthusiasm from the potential funder. If you show a disinterested attitude, even if there are potential pitfalls, you are unlikely to gain support. Do not be afraid to 'blow your own trumpet'. Your track record is important and if you have achieved something special, tell the funder. They cannot know unless you tell them.

Knowing your subject

To succeed with your business you must know all about the market and the opportunities as well as the risks involved. There are always risks involved with all businesses but these can always be minimised. Make sure you recognise the potential risks and then you will be able to tell the funder what you propose to do to deal with them.

Hopefully you will have covered all of these in your business plan but, if the funder raises other risks that you have not considered, by having full knowledge of your subject area you should be able to answer their questions.

Being truthful in your answers

Telling the truth is absolutely vital to your integrity and to your reputation. If you attempt to mislead the potential funder by misrepresenting the facts you will damage your chances of gaining funding. If you do not know the answer to any question that the funder has then say so. Do not attempt to waffle. It is better to recognise that they may have considered something that you have not.

If this does happen, it will hopefully be to do with a peripheral area of your project. This should not affect your chances of gaining funding providing you find out the answer fairly quickly. If, however, the question concerns a major area of your proposal it is obviously something that you should have considered before. You will more than likely be sent away with the advice that you should reconsider your entire project.

Making sure that you understand the forecasts

This is an area where a lot of business owners come unstuck. The financial forecasts are prepared by their accountant who will probably also attend the meeting with the funder. When questions arise on these forecasts the business owner then defers to the accountant to answer. The funder, however, requires the answers from you. It is your business and it is vitally important that you understand what the forecasts reveal.

Whilst you can use the expertise of the accountant in modelling the various relevant forecasts, it is you who will take the final decision as to the suitability, feasibility and acceptability of those forecasts. It is always necessary to make assumptions in forecasts and such assumptions, and the reasons behind them, must be understood by you. Unless the funder can be convinced that you have total control of your finances it is unlikely that they will be willing to support you.

FIRST IMPRESSIONS COUNT

From the moment you meet the potential funder they will be making an assessment of you. There is one golden rule – always smile at them and look confident. Starting your own business requires confidence in your own ability to be successful and you must exude this confidence in your attitude.

You do, however, need to temper this so that you do not appear over-confident or even cocky. You are asking the funder to make an investment in your business and they must be convinced that you have the right attitude and ability to succeed.

Being on time

Always be on time for an appointment. The funder will have allocated a certain amount of time to discuss your plans and if you are late you are merely eroding the time that will be available to you.

It is always a good idea to be early, although not too early, for your appointment.

Allow yourself plenty of time to get there and at the very least aim to arrive ten minutes early. This serves a number of purposes:

- It allows you time to gather your thoughts and prepare yourself mentally.

- It avoids arriving flustered which will not help with first impressions.

- It demonstrates that you can organise your time effectively.

- It may increase the time you can spend with the funder because they may see you earlier than the appointed time.

Dressing appropriately

It does not matter what sort of business you are starting. You still need to convey an image of professionalism. That does not mean that you have to go out and buy a suit specially for the occasion. It means that you must not attend in workshop overalls, looking grimy and with filthy hands. You can still look smart in casual clothes.

KNOWING WHAT THEY LOOK FOR

Risk assessment is founded on a set of principles, one of the acronyms for which is CAMPARI. This stands for Character, Ability, Means, Purpose, Amount, Repayment and Insurance.

Understanding exactly how a funder will make an assessment of your proposition will give you a greater chance of success. It will also give you food for thought before you present your proposition to ensure that all aspects are covered.

Character

If your character has been blemished in any way as a result of previous business dealings, you will face an uphill struggle to raise funds. For a funder, an unblemished character is vital. It will not make any difference how good your proposal is, without proven honesty and integrity the proposal will more than likely be declined for this one simple reason.

The funder will want to be sure that your word is reliable, not just on the basic details of the proposition, but also on the repayment proposals. If you have previously made exaggerated claims that proved to be over-optimistic and led to a delay in repayment, this will make any funder extremely wary of your new proposals.

Ability

The funder will want to be sure that you have the necessary skills to run a business. They will need to be satisfied with your management skills and experience, together with such factors as your state of health and the energy and enthusiasm that you possess.

Whilst they will recognise that you may be lacking in some management areas, they will need to see that you are willing to do something about this. This could take the form of management training of some kind, or, in some circumstances, the appointment of new members to your management team.

Means

In this context means refers to your net assets. The extent of your means will give an indication to the funder of your past performance and success as an entrepreneur. Be aware, however, that inherited wealth will give no such indication. This merely relates to the success of your family.

The liquid means of both the entrepreneur and the business are of importance to the funder. They will need to be convinced in all cases that short-term liabilities can be paid from short-term assets. One of the questions that may be asked, in the absence of such short-term cover, is how readily assets can be turned into cash.

Purpose

There are a number of factors that the funder will consider when looking at the purpose of your proposed borrowing. All but perhaps the first of these should already have been considered by you:

- necessity
- suitability
- feasibility
- acceptability.

Some requests for borrowing are made on a contingency basis. In other words, the money is not actually required but you are seeking a cushion in case something goes wrong. If you make a request for funding on this speculative basis it is very unlikely that you will receive a positive response.

Suitability relates to the compatibility of the purpose of your request. It also relates to whether the type of funding you have requested is suitable for the purpose. For example, an overdraft facility is for short-term working capital requirements whereas a loan is more appropriate for long-term investment in fixed assets.

Unless the purpose of the borrowing request is considered entirely feasible in relation to your business it will be turned down. For example, you may have overlooked potential problems that could have an adverse impact on your business. Under these circumstances it is actually in your best interests that the proposition is declined.

Acceptability can take a number of forms. For example, the purpose may be unacceptable to the funder on policy grounds. The purpose may be prohibited by law, for example the financing of arms shipments to certain countries. Acceptability of the purpose, provided it is legal, could be a subjective issue and will differ from funder to funder.

Amount

This question has two aspects: how much is required from the funder and how much are you investing in your business? A balance is required in terms of the contribution from both you and the funder. You should be risking sufficient money in the business and unless you are making an adequate contribution your proposition is likely to be declined.

A further point that the funder will consider is whether the correct amount is being requested. Is it too much, or is it not enough? There are inherent dangers in either situation especially where too little is requested. This could mean, for example, that whilst your original project was acceptable, based on the amount requested, it could turn into an unacceptable project if the amount was increased through unforeseen circumstances.

The danger in this to both you and the funder is where an insufficient amount is requested from the bank and you have no other cash resources to inject to solve any problem. This would mean that if the funder declined the application for further funding the original project, probably now partially completed, would be placed in jeopardy.

Repayment

The funder will need to be satisfied that your business will have the ability to repay the borrowed funds. At least in the short-term, positive cash flow will be crucial because in the absence of cash you will be unable to meet your liabilities and your business could very quickly fail.

When assessing your repayment ability, the funder will look at two key areas:

- The source – exactly where repayment will be coming from.
- Timing – exactly when the funder will be fully repaid.

Being able to make repayment when it is expected is really the key to your whole proposition. Unless you can convince the funder on this aspect, all of the other principles of lending do not matter. You can have the character, means, and ability to run the business but unless you can make repayment of the debt when it is due you will not gain the funding.

Insurance

In the context of the assessment of a lending proposition, insurance relates to the security in the form of assets that you can offer to support your request for funding. There are a number of different types of security that the bank will consider. The implications involved in giving security and the types of security generally taken are looked at in detail in Chapter 5.

WORKING OUT THE COST

The cost of borrowing money can soon mount up when all the various charges and interest are added together. You need to be aware that most funders have guidelines, or target rates, that they will aim to achieve. Just like any other business they have their own business objectives and they will aim to charge as much as they can.

This does not mean, however, that you have to accept the first rate that is offered. All charges and interest rates are negotiable. It will be up to you to use your skills of negotiation to obtain the best deal for your business. Competition is intense within the financial services sector and when starting your business you should obtain a number of quotations. You also need to advise each funder that you are doing this in order that, hopefully, they will give you their lowest quote for your business.

Interest rates

Interest rates will vary widely depending on whether or not security for the debt is available. They can be quoted in a number of different ways, for example:

- variable
- fixed
- managed
- annual percentage.

Variable
Rates quoted in this way are usually linked to what is known as base rate. A lender's base rate is usually the same as the Bank of England base rate although there can be variations. An additional margin of anywhere between 1% and 7% is added to the base rate and this will be the rate that is quoted.

Fixed
Fixed rates are usually offered for long-term lending and they remain the same throughout the term of the loan. Whether you choose a fixed rate or not will depend on your view of how base rate is likely to move during the period of the loan. If, for example, rates are comparatively high when you take out the loan you may not wish to be locked into a high fixed rate. The danger that you face, of course, is that the rate will move even higher.

Managed
This is a confusing method of quoting interest rates that unfortunately is being used more and more by funders. The rate is fixed, but it can be changed if the funder wishes. You really need to consider this type of rate as being variable because it can be changed overnight.

Annual percentage
This is the one rate that you can use to compare any other form of interest rate that you are quoted. It is required to be quoted by law, no matter how the rate is to be calculated. It is referred to as the annual percentage rate and often abbreviated to APR. Before you sign any agreement to borrow money you should check the APR carefully to avoid nasty surprises later.

Interest rates are often quoted and charged on a monthly basis and it can come as a shock to discover the true cost of borrowing the money. As an example, a quoted monthly rate of 1.5% does not sound very much until you realise that the actual true APR is probably in the region of 20% on an annualised basis.

Paying arrangement fees

As part of the cost of borrowing money you can expect to pay an **arrangement fee**. This fee is charged to cover the costs of setting up the funding and administering the debt over the repayment period. The amount of this fee is generally linked as a percentage of the overall funding package. Accordingly you can expect to be charged an additional 1% to 2% for a loan.

In the case of a bank overdraft, the fee is usually fixed according to how much you require. As examples, an overdraft of up to £3,000 may incur a minimum arrangement fee of £85 and for an overdraft between £3,000 and £5,000 a fee of £110 will be payable.

Paying transmission charges

If you are approaching a bank for start-up finance you will also need to consider other charges that will be payable for running your account. These are generally referred to as **transmission charges**.

Virtually all the high street banks offer special deals on transmission charges for new businesses with 'free' banking being offered for limited periods. These usually last from anything from the first 12 months of trading up to the first two years. Depending on the size of your business these can be a quite considerable cost and you need to make careful comparisons as to what is available.

KEY POINTS

- Always put yourself in the shoes of the potential funder – ask yourself if you would lend money to support this business.

- Prepare yourself fully for the potential meeting with a funder – make sure you understand your business plan and the related financial forecasts thoroughly.

- Never be late for an appointment – remember first impressions count.

- Make sure that your funding proposal is comprehensive by using the basic principles of risk assessment.

- Look at the costs involved with borrowing money – take into account all fees and charges and not just the quoted interest rate.

4

Using Your Bank

A bank can provide you with a large amount of information on starting a business. The high street banks all provide information packs in one form or another. Some will even provide you with computer software to help you write your business plan and compile financial forecasts.

A good relationship with a bank is essential if your business is to prosper. Unfortunately, a lot of the high street banks are no longer offering a personalised service to small start-up businesses. You may find that you never see the same person twice and indeed you will not have the level of support that larger businesses are afforded.

It will therefore pay you to make your choice of bank carefully. Banking is an extremely competitive industry and you must find out as much information as you can about the services offered.

MAKING IT YOUR FIRST PORT OF CALL

You do not need to have an account with a bank to go and talk to them about your plans for a business. Indeed I would suggest that you go and see as many as you can. This will help you in making your final choice as to where you want to open an account. Only once you are satisfied with the potential level of service that you will receive should you open an account. By this stage you should also have been able to gauge whether the bank is likely to offer you financial support.

Using their business information facility

As already stated, most of the high street banks will have specific packs designed to help you think through the process of starting your business. In addition, some of the banks offer a business information facility. This consists of a tailored directory, based on your postcode, providing up-to-date information on other sources of finance, training and advisory services that are available to you.

The information pack can also, wherever possible, provide a profile of the type of business you are aiming to start, with specific information on the typical market and customers together with competition and start-up costs. In addition, guidance is provided on subjects such as tax and National Insurance, VAT concerns and a wealth of other useful information. The best part of this information service is that it is provided free of charge so make sure you take advantage of it.

Asking their opinion

Before you put any formal request for funding to a bank it is worthwhile seeking an informal discussion on your plans. The bank is very likely to have existing customers operating in the same market and they may be able to give you advice on areas that you had not previously considered.

The bank can also help you to put your initial thoughts for your business into a more formal structure. Remember, if you are going to be asking for their support it is better to put your proposal into a format that they can easily work with. The bank will also be able to point you in the direction of other people or organisations that can help you. Never be afraid to ask for help. You may be eligible for grants or other assistance and the bank can give you specific advice on who you should be approaching.

Gaining their support

There is no doubt that the vast majority of funds lent to small businesses is provided by the high street banks. All banks offer a wide variety of specialist lending schemes aimed at the small business market, each tailored to suit the needs of the individual business.

For this very reason if you need to borrow money to finance your new business the first funder that you should approach will be the bank. Unless you can gain the support of your bank to finance your business, at least in part, it is unlikely that you will gain funding from any other source.

In Chapter 2 we looked at the sorts of finance available for both short-term and long-term requirements and we can now look in more detail at the options that are available to you.

WORKING WITH AN OVERDRAFT

The simplest and indeed the most flexible form of bank funding is by way of an overdraft. In simple terms, a limit is agreed for a defined period during which you may borrow money up to that limit. It is extremely important that you remember that an overdraft is short-term finance. The limit may be agreed for any period from six months up to one year but it is there to provide working capital.

Never, under any circumstances, use an overdraft facility as a replacement for long-term finance. If you need to purchase fixed assets or other items to be used in the long-term you must arrange more appropriate finance.

The concept of the working capital facility

It is essential that you understand the concept of the working capital facility, or, in other words, the overdraft facility. The working capital in your business is defined as your current assets less your current liabilities. It is critical that your current assets are always greater than your current liabilities. Unless they are you may be unable to meet your short-term liabilities when they become payable.

For this reason you need to have tight control over the components of working capital within your business and the overdraft facility will help in this respect. It will enable you to pay your creditors on time pending receipt of funds from your debtors.

Keeping it under control

It is vitally important that you keep your overdraft under control. Remember that this type of bank borrowing is repayable upon demand and if you abuse the facility it may be withdrawn at any time. Quite apart from this, exceeding the agreed limit can be extremely costly in terms of financial penalties.

It is quite common for a penal rate of interest to be applied to any borrowing over the agreed facility and this could be in excess of 30% per annum. It will not matter that a rate of interest has been agreed for the facility, the excess amount that you are overdrawn over and above this figure has not been agreed.

This also presupposes that the bank will actually allow you to exceed the agreed amount. If it is necessary for the bank to return items such as cheques, standing orders, or direct debits in order to control your overdraft then you can expect to incur a fee of around £30 for each item.

You must never allow this to happen. If you lose control over your finances you have lost control of your business. You are no longer making payments as and when they fall due. The bank is being forced to decide what items should be paid from your account and those that should not.

Offsetting the interest

If you operate more than one account with a bank you may find that in some circumstances you can arrange a **group account** facility. This is where the accounts are linked together in the bank's books and the overall balance of the combined accounts is utilised for the calculation of interest. For obvious reasons this is only beneficial to you when you have at least one account in the group that is in credit.

Most banks will not openly offer this facility to you. You may have to make a specific request for it to be put in place. Additionally, the bank will usually impose what is referred to as a **turn**. This is a charge of 1% or 2% on the amount of the overdraft that is being offset by credit balances. The criteria for offsetting your overdraft will vary from bank to bank and you need to make your own enquiries if you consider that such a facility would be useful.

SEEKING A LOAN

All banks offer business loans under a variety of different product names. At this stage it is perhaps worthwhile pointing out that, as with all businesses, the bank is there to sell their products and services. You can be sure that the bank manager will have his own performance targets and some of these will be directly linked to the products and services that they can offer. It is entirely a matter for you to make sure that the product or service you purchase is exactly what you want.

Some banks also offer special loan deals for businesses that are starting up. Despite the fact that these will offer some concessions on the interest rate and arrangement fee that will be charged, you do need to check that they are actually the best deal that you can get. Some of these loans are only offered on fixed terms whereas you may actually prefer to borrow on a variable rate basis. Both fixed rate and variable rate loans are considered in greater detail later in this chapter.

Loans are usually subject to a minimum amount of £1,000 and a maximum amount of £1m. Repayment terms are also flexible, depending upon the purpose of the loan, and can range from a 12-month period up to 20 years.

In some circumstances it is also possible to arrange a **capital repayment holiday** where only the interest needs to be repaid for the defined term of the holiday. This can be advantageous for a new business in that it keeps expenditure down to a minimum whilst income is being built up from trade. This type of deferred repayment should be available no matter whether you opt for a fixed rate or a variable rate loan.

Using long-term funding

Gaining long-term funding is absolutely essential for major capital expenditure. As an example, you would never consider buying your house using anything other than a long-term mortgage loan. You must use the same principle in your business.

In the same way, as mentioned earlier you should never consider borrowing money for any term other than that linked to the life of the asset that you were purchasing. When you come to replace the asset at the end of its useful life it will be fully paid for and you can start the process again. You do not want to be in a position of scrapping some equipment but still actually having a loan outstanding which has yet to be repaid.

Using variable rate loans

Variable rate loans are entirely flexible, but you need to be aware that this can actually cause you problems especially if base lending rate increases. The bank will usually review your outstanding loan on an annual basis and, if base rate has increased substantially during the past 12 months, this can also lead to a substantial increase in your repayments.

On the other hand, the bank may be willing to extend the repayment time-scale to allow you additional time to pay off the loan. Either way your costs have increased and this can only come out of your business profits. It can also make budgeting very difficult.

If you are arranging a variable rate loan for a substantial amount, generally a minimum of £100,000, you may be able to arrange what is called a **rate cap**. This is an agreement to limit the interest rate costs to a maximum level should base rate increases be imposed. This 'cap' will be for a specific period and there will be a premium for you to pay. It is, in effect, an insurance policy that will cover the situation should base rate changes move against you.

Using fixed rate loans

Fixed rate loans have three specific features which are designed to take away the uncertainty of using a variable rate loan:

- The interest rate for the entire period of the loan is fixed from the outset.

- The monthly repayments are also then fixed for the full term of the loan.

- The full term of the loan is also then fixed.

This means that you know from the outset exactly how much your repayments will be each month and how long the loan will take to repay. Neither of these can vary throughout the entire period of the loan. As you might expect, however, there can be a financial cost for this certainty.

It is likely that the interest rate that you will be offered will be higher than a comparative interest rate for a variable rate loan. Remember that by offering the fixed rate the bank is having to make assumptions about how base rate is likely to move in the future. In effect this additional cost is the premium that you have to pay to ensure financial stability.

If the loan is only over a short period, say to a maximum term of two years, then you need to consider whether you actually need this protection against interest rate increases. Depending on the amount of the loan it may be worth the risk of opting for a variable rate loan, on the basis that even if interest rates do increase the additional cost may be minimal. I can offer you no clear guidance on which type of loan is best. It will depend on the circumstances. Only you can decide on the best possible option for your business.

Loan repayment tables

To help you establish the repayments necessary for any loan, two tables appear in Figure 5 with various interest rates and repayment terms. In order to work out the monthly repayment for a loan you merely take the relevant cost from the table and multiply this figure by the amount of the loan that you require.

Please remember that these repayment tables can only provide a general guide to the repayments that will be required. The actual repayment amount will be based on when the bank charges the interest to the loan account. Some loans are charged interest monthly and others are charged quarterly. This is, of course,

Years		Interest rates				
	10%	11%	12%	13%	14%	15%
1	£87.92	£88.38	£88.85	£89.32	£89.79	£90.26
2	£46.14	£46.61	£47.07	£47.54	£48.01	£48.49
3	£32.27	£32.74	£33.21	£33.69	£34.18	£34.67
4	£25.36	£25.85	£26.33	£26.83	£27.33	£27.83
5	£21.25	£21.74	£22.24	£22.75	£23.27	£23.79
6	£18.53	£19.03	£19.55	£20.07	£20.61	£21.15
7	£16.60	£17.12	£17.65	£18.19	£18.74	£19.30
8	£15.17	£15.71	£16.25	£16.81	£17.37	£17.95
9	£14.08	£14.63	£15.18	£15.75	£16.33	£16.92
10	£13.22	£13.78	£14.35	£14.93	£15.53	£16.13

Years		Interest rates				
	16%	17%	18%	19%	20%	21%
1	£90.73	£91.20	£91.68	£92.16	£92.63	£93.11
2	£48.96	£49.44	£49.92	£50.41	£50.90	£51.39
3	£35.16	£35.65	£36.15	£36.66	£37.16	£37.68
4	£28.34	£28.86	£29.37	£29.90	£30.43	£30.97
5	£24.32	£24.85	£25.39	£25.94	£26.49	£27.05
6	£21.69	£22.25	£22.81	£23.38	£23.95	£24.54
7	£19.86	£20.44	£21.02	£21.61	£22.21	£22.81
8	£18.53	£19.12	£19.72	£20.33	£20.95	£21.58
9	£17.53	£18.14	£18.76	£19.39	£20.03	£20.67
10	£16.75	£17.38	£18.02	£18.67	£19.33	£19.99

- The repayment amount for a loan of £8,600 repayble over ten years at an interest rate of 12% = 8.6 x £14.35 = £123.41 per month.

Fig. 5. Monthly repayments calculator.

another aspect that you will need to consider when you are pricing the true cost of the loan.

As covered in Chapter 3 you can only make a direct comparison of the true costs of borrowing money when you know the APR.

UTILISING A BANK SUBSIDIARY

Most banks have a number of subsidiaries covering a wide variety of financial services. Examples include:

- leasing and hire purchase
- factoring
- insurance and pensions
- mortgages.

Remember that the bank will only normally offer their own products. As with all purchases that you make you will still need to shop around to get the best deal for your business. By obtaining a quotation for a particular product it will, at least, give you a starting point in order to make comparisons.

Gaining an introduction

You will have little trouble in gaining an introduction from your bank manager to one of the bank's subsidiaries. It is more than likely that the bank manager will, in fact, have specific performance related targets in this respect. I would, indeed, be very surprised if the bank manager did not offer an introduction to at least one subsidiary, probably for insurance and pension advice, without your even making a request.

Protecting the debt

If you are starting your business, and borrowing money to do so, there is one important factor that you need to consider under three different scenarios. How will you make the repayments and gain an income:

- If you are involved in an accident?
- If you are diagnosed with a life-threatening illness?
- In the event of your sudden death?

As a sole trader your only source of income is from your business efforts and, if you suddenly find that you cannot work, you need to have some sort of protection by way of insurance cover. At this stage I should caution you against using a **loan protection policy** that may be offered by your bank when you take out a loan. These can, by comparison, be extremely expensive forms of insurance cover. I would strongly recommend that you seek alternative quotations for specific insurance policies covering the three scenarios outlined above.

Accident and sickness
You need to arrange an alternative income in the event of an unfortunate accident or short-term sickness. These policies will pay out a monthly amount and for obvious reasons you need to arrange sufficient insurance to ensure that the income will cover your expenditure. These policies should be reviewed annually and the insurance cover increased accordingly.

Critical illness
These policies will pay out a lump sum in the event of you being diagnosed with a life-threatening illness. In many ways they are similar to life policies but the lump sum is paid out as soon as a diagnosis is made. Payment is not dependent upon your death and, should you survive the illness, the lump sum is not repayable.

Death
It is relatively inexpensive to arrange a term life assurance policy for an adequate sum to pay off all your debts. This is something that you need to consider extremely carefully, especially if you have a family. Always remember that, in the absence of sufficient insurance cover, your debts will have to be met from your estate. This may involve the sale of assets that you own which are also an important part of your family's life.

Looking after your future
The final section of this chapter covers an area that most people, especially young people who are starting their own business, do not take seriously. A pension. At some stage in your life, unless you want to carry on working until you die, you will want to retire. It is absolutely essential that you start making plans for your pension as early as possible. The greater number of years and contributions that you make to a pension plan the larger your pension fund will be.

The longer you leave establishing a pension for yourself the smaller the eventual fund will be and the smaller the monthly income. Take my advice and consider making pension contributions as soon as you start your business. Even if it means making cost savings in other areas of your expenditure you will reap the rewards when it comes to retirement.

KEY POINTS

- A bank is a useful source of information on starting and funding your own business – make sure that you obtain one of their specialist business packs.

- Understand the concept of a working capital overdraft facility and do not abuse it by using it to purchase fixed assets.

- Make sure that you stay within any agreed overdraft facility – the penalties for exceeding the limit can be very expensive.

- Choose carefully between accepting a fixed rate loan and a variable rate loan – do not forget that the interest rate is negotiable.

- Always take out adequate insurance to not only protect the debt but also to provide you with an income should you find yourself unable to work.

5

Considering a Request for Security

Depending upon the amount of funding you are seeking, and the risk assessment made by the potential funder, you may find that some form of **security** for the borrowing is requested. In this chapter we will look at the types of security that are generally requested and, in the final section, an alternative type of security that is supported by backing from the Department of Trade and Industry.

You should consider a request for security very carefully but, if you are to demonstrate total commitment to your business, you should not be put off from granting the request if you are able. You must realise that whilst the funder will accept a modicum of risk, the business is yours and therefore the majority of the risk should sit on your shoulders.

KNOWING THE IMPLICATIONS

Security is required by a funder to act as a potential insurance policy should things go wrong. They will be looking for assets that have three important attributes; that can be easily:

- made subject to a legal charge
- valued on a current basis
- sold in the event of default.

From these three attributes you can easily understand the implications of granting security for a debt. If the debt is not repaid as arranged, the assets will be seized and sold by the funder to gain repayment. It is as simple as that.

Is the request reasonable?

Some funders have clear internal guidelines as to when a request for security should be made whatever the proposition. For some types of funding, for example hire purchase, the asset that is purchased is used as the security for the debt. There can be no clear guidelines as to whether a request for security is reasonable. It should depend entirely upon the proposition. Consider the following two hypothetical situations:

- A loan of £50,000 is required towards a total business funding proposal of £60,000. In this case a request for security would be entirely appropriate, the majority of the risk is falling on the funder.

- An overdraft of £5,000 is required to cover short-term working capital where the owner of the business has already invested £25,000 to start the business. A request for security in this case would probably be inappropriate.

You will need to decide for yourself whether the request is reasonable and, if necessary, arrange a different package of funding. If you are purchasing assets to be used in the business this is made a lot easier by opting to use a finance company. This aspect is looked at in greater detail in the next chapter.

Considering your family

If you have a family they may be a large consideration as to whether or not security should be given, especially when it takes the form of a mortgage over the family home. Always remember the implications outlined above. If your business fails the family home will be sold to repay the debt.

Before granting the mortgage you will need to be absolutely sure that your business proposals are sound and secure. The funder wants to see you succeed but, if things do go wrong, they will have no compunction in seizing your assets. They will not accept a bad debt lightly and will make every effort to pursue you for repayment. It is essential, therefore, that you have the total commitment of your spouse or partner to your business. They will need to be convinced that the risks of losing their home will be minimal.

What if the business fails?

Having emphasised in the previous section the risks involved in granting security, the funder will only take such steps if there is no alternative. In the final chapter in this book we will look at some of the ways in which you can deal with difficulties. For the moment, however, let us assume that the business has failed totally and still owes money to creditors, including a funder to whom security has been granted.

The critically important piece of advice that I can give is that you must face up to the situation. You cannot ignore the position in which you find yourself and hope that it will go away. If you do this you will inevitably lose everything. Your first step must be to seek some alternative way in which to earn an income. If you can make an acceptable alternative repayment programme for your debts it is unlikely that the funder holding the security will actually attempt to realise it.

Realisation of security will always be the funder's final option. They have no wish to encounter possible bad publicity in the event of a forced sale of the family home. When you encounter a situation that is likely to cause your business to fail you must seek help and advice from the funder. If you talk to them they will be sympathetic.

MORTGAGING YOUR HOUSE

Your house is likely to be the greatest asset that you own although it may already be the subject of a mortgage. The funder will require full details of exactly who owns the house, be it in your sole name or with a partner and, more importantly, who actually lives in it. The reason for this is that the property may be occupied by someone who does not actually own it but by living in the property they may have a legal vested interest.

The funder will require a number of formalities to be completed before they will lend any money against the security quite apart from the signing of a legal mortgage. If it is a second mortgage they will require full details of the first mortgage together with confirmation that repayments on that mortgage are up to date. The funder will also want to ensure that the property is adequately insured against fire and other risks.

Valuing the house

In some circumstances the funder may require a full professional valuation to be obtained. In the majority of cases the funder will make a personal visit to ensure that the property is in a reasonable condition and suitable as security. Once the valuation has been obtained the funder will then usually discount this value by between 10% and 30%. The reason for this is to allow a contingency factor and provide for the costs of sale should it be necessary for the property to be sold to repay the debt.

If you are not actually occupying the property yourself, for example it may be a holiday cottage that you rent out to visitors, the property valuation may be discounted by as much as 55%. In all cases any prior mortgage is then deducted from the residual value to calculate a valuation of the security. This may seem harsh but, if the funder does take possession, they will not want a protracted sale. It must value the property and indeed offer it for sale at a price that will ensure a quick disposal.

Meeting the costs of the mortgage

The funder will require you to meet all the external costs of taking the mortgage, together with a security fee to cover their own administrative costs. These can be quite substantial and involve:

- professional valuation fee
- local authority and Land Registry searches
- report on title if the land is unregistered
- solicitor's fees
- Land Registry registration fee.

Some of these are linked to the value of the property, for example the Land Registry registration fee, and others will be approximately the same for all properties. By the time you add them all together, however, you can be looking at a minimum of £500 in costs.

Understanding the effects of the mortgage

If it is a first mortgage there are no effects that need to concern you other than the risk of losing your home through non-payment of the debt. If it is a second mortgage, however, the new mortgage will affect your relationship with the holder of the first mortgage.

The most important effect is that you will not be able to obtain any further funding from the holder of the first mortgage without the consent of the second mortgagor. For obvious reasons the second mortgagor will not let you borrow any more money which, as a consequence, would reduce the value of their mortgage.

You also need to be aware that if you are having problems meeting the repayments on the first mortgage, the holder of that mortgage will pass on this information to the holder of the second mortgage. They will, in effect, work together to protect the value of their security. If you are having problems in this regard it is better to reveal this to the holder of the second mortgage, and discuss ways in which it will be resolved, rather than let the second mortgage holder hear about it from the first mortgagor.

MORTGAGING YOUR BUSINESS

If you intend to operate your business through the auspices of a limited liability company it is possible to mortgage all the assets of the business. This will take the form of a mortgage debenture and, quite apart from mortgaging the assets, it will give the funder various legal rights of which you need to be aware.

The most important of these is that it will enable the funder to appoint an administrative receiver in the event of default. The reason for this is that the funder will want to be sure that at the time of default all available assets will be secured. One way that the funder can do this is to appoint a receiver who is well known and trusted to also act to protect the funder's position.

The effects of a mortgage debenture

By signing a mortgage debenture you are granting a fixed and floating charge over all of the business's assets. A legal mortgage over all your property will be included and an equitable mortgage over all your other assets, for example plant, machinery and stock. Effectively you will be unable to dispose of any of your business assets without prior permission.

You are also making a number of other commitments. The two most important are likely to be:

- That all money received in the course of trade is to be placed through an account held with the funder.

- You may not sell, factor, or discount your book debts, i.e. your debtors, without the consent of the funder.

Valuing the business assets

As with a property valuation the assets of the business are valued on a forced sale, or break-up basis. If the business does fail it is unlikely that the assets can be sold at anywhere near their book valuation. Industrial premises are usually valued on the following basis:

- first mortgage – 70% of the open market valuation (OMV)
- second mortgage – 45% of the OMV less the first mortgage.

The valuations placed on other assets of the business will vary but for general guidance purposes the following percentages of the accounting book values are used by funders:

- plant and machinery – 20%
- stock in hand – 30%
- debtors – 60%.

In addition, it is usual to only allow debtors into the calculation where the debt has been outstanding for less than 90 days. Any debtors outstanding in excess of that length of time are considered as potentially bad.

OFFERING OTHER TYPES OF SECURITY

A funder may accept all sorts of tangible security provided they meet the three essential attributes discussed at the start of this chapter.

Life policies

In most cases these will be endowment policies that are capable of being surrendered to obtain money to repay the debt. For large debts the funder may also insist upon a term assurance policy with a sufficient sum assured to repay the debt in the event of the borrower's death.

There are very few formalities involved in taking a life policy as security. The funder will need to ensure that:

- a form of legal mortgage is signed
- premiums are paid to date
- a current surrender value is obtained
- the policy is 'age admitted'.

This last formality is necessary because most life insurance companies will not pay out under a policy unless proof of age of the life assured has been seen. This merely involves sending a certified copy of the appropriate birth certificate to the insurance company for registration in their records.

Stocks and shares

Security in the form of stocks and shares is also sometimes accepted as an option by a funder. In the majority of cases a legal mortgage is signed and the ownership of the holding is transferred to a funder's nominee company. The stocks and shares do, however, need to be easily sold to be acceptable and for this reason they will need to be quoted on a recognised stock exchange.

In view of the volatility of the stock markets, the market value is generally written down to 60% for the purposes of the security valuation. In addition, to provide a further cushion, the funder may insist upon an extra margin of 25% over and above the level of borrowing.

It sounds complicated but a specific example will help. A portfolio of stocks and shares is held which when valued on a stock market basis amounts to £20,000. The value for security purposes is therefore £12,000, although this will only support borrowing up to a maximum of £9,000 being 75% of the security value.

Giving guarantees

A guarantee is quite simply a promise by one person to meet the debts of another should the original borrower default on repayment. Guarantees are commonly taken from company directors where the borrowing is in the name of a limited liability company. This is, effectively, to allow the funder to get around the provisions of the limited liability.

Not only is the company liable for its debts, but where a guarantee is taken from the directors they also become personally liable. Depending upon the amount of the borrowing it may be necessary for the funder to seek tangible security to support the promise to pay. This security can take any of the forms already considered.

USING THE SMALL FIRMS LOAN GUARANTEE SCHEME

What is it?

The Small Firms Loan Guarantee Scheme (SFLGS) is a joint venture operated by the Small Business Service (SBS) and a consortium of lenders including the high street banks (see Figure 6). It is available to small businesses that have a viable business plan but who have been unable to raise a conventional loan. This may be because of a lack of security or a business track record, or both.

Under the scheme the government provides a guarantee to the participating funder against default by the borrower. The amount of

Small Firms Loan Guarantee Scheme – Small Loans Arrangements
Customer Detail Form

My Bank Plc _____

Branch Address _____

Full Name of Applicant(s) _____

Trading Name (if different from above) _____

Amount £ _____

Drawdown Date [ ] [ ]

Fixed Rate _____ %

Variable Rate _____ %

Guarantee Premium Rate _____

Term of Loan _____ Years (maximum 10 years)

Date of Final Repayment _____

Length of Capital Repayment Holiday 6/12/24* Months

*Delete as appropriate

Guarantee Level _____

Purpose of Loan _____

Trading Address _____

_____

Legal Status (Delete as applicable)

Sole Trader/Partnership/Limited Company/Unlimited Company/

Industrial and Provident Society/Co-operative

Registered Office (if applicable) _____

Full names of Shareholders/Members (if applicable)

_____

Full names of Partners/Directors/Members (if applicable)

_____

Existing and Proposed Facilities from Bank

	Existing (£)	Proposed (£)
Overdraft		
Loans		
Other Liabilities		

Business SIC Code _____

Main Activities _____

Is the Loan for a new business? **Yes/No** (Delete as applicable)

62

Number of Employees

– now _____

– forecast in 12 months _____

– has the business been trading continuously for two years or more immediately prior to this application? **Yes/No**

If **yes**, evidence is needed to satisfy the Lender as to the length of the trading period (list) _____

Turnover

– for last 12 months _____

– forecast in 12 months _____

Has the Applicant (or Partners/Directors/Members) previously borrowed or been associated with a borrower under the Scheme at any time? **Yes/No**
(Delete as applicable)

If **Yes** – give details _____

Existing and
Proposed Facilities
from other Banks

Declaration
The Applicant warrants that the information given is complete and accurate.

Disclosure Authority
For the purpose of the Small Firms Loan Guarantee Scheme I/we authorise My Bank Plc to disclose to the Secretary of State, or his Agent(s), any information which My Bank Plc may have relating to

_____ (Name of Account)

Signed by _____ (in accordance with the Bank Mandate)

For Lender Use Only

Sanctioned _____ Name _____ Date _____

(Signature)

Note to Branches: Please ensure that a copy of this form is sent to Small Business Services immediately the loan is drawn down.

Fig. 6. Application form for the Small Firms Loan Guarantee Scheme.

this guarantee is 70% of the loan, although for businesses that have been trading for more than two years this increases to 85%. This therefore mitigates substantially the risk that the funder is taking in granting the loan.

The minimum amount of loan that can be considered is £5,000 and for a new start business the maximum is £100,000. For established businesses that have been trading for at least two years the maximum amount available rises to £250,000. Guarantees are available to cover loans repayable between two and ten years.

Who can use it?

The scheme is open to all types of businesses be they:

- sole traders
- partnerships
- limited liability companies
- co-operatives.

In terms of eligible business activities these cover a wide variety of goods and services, including all manufacturing and construction firms and many service industries.

There are, however, a number of restrictions that apply in actually classifying a business as 'small'. In addition, there are a number of business activities where specific restrictions may apply depending on the circumstances. In some cases, specifically in the retail sector, no businesses are eligible for the scheme at all. You will need to check the current criteria when you make your application. A brochure outlining the scheme in full is available free of charge from the Small Business Service.

What does it cost?

There are three components involved in the total cost of loans obtained under the SFLGS.

Interest

The interest rate on the loan will be subject to negotiation although in view of the guarantee will be subject to preferential terms. It will also depend on whether you opt for a fixed interest rate or a variable interest rate. The commercial decision on this aspect, as before, is down to you.

Arrangement fee
The funder will charge you a fee to establish the loan. This arrangement fee will depend upon the funder but will generally be in the range of 1% to 1.5% of the total amount of the loan.

SBS premium
The SBS also charges a premium on the outstanding amount of the loan throughout the repayment term. The amount will depend upon whether the loan is taken on fixed rate or variable rate interest terms:

- variable rate – 1.5% per annum
- fixed rate – 0.5% per annum.

For loans of over £30,000 the premium is paid quarterly throughout the term of the loan. For loans of £30,000 or under, the premium is paid in full at the outset.

KEY POINTS

- Make sure you understand the exact implications of granting security to a funder in the event of the failure of your business.

- You will need the full support and commitment of your family if you mortgage your house to provide security for your business debts.

- If you operate your business as a limited liability company you do have the option of offering a mortgage debenture as security.

- Consider using the Small Firms Loan Guarantee Scheme – it is still available even if you have other personal assets that could be used as security.

6

Looking at Finance Company Options

If you require funding for the purchase of assets, for example plant and machinery or tools and equipment, there are further options that you can consider. Some of these offer a number of advantages over obtaining a loan for the purchase of such assets.

By looking at these alternatives you can also protect your business from purchasing assets that are quickly made obsolete by advances in technology, for example computer equipment. Many of these options can also have a positive impact on the gearing ratio for the overall funding package because they will be excluded from the equation.

In many ways obtaining funding from a finance company can actually be easier to obtain than a traditional bank loan. The reason for this is that in some instances the asset can be used as security for the debt and in others the ownership of the asset is not actually vested in you.

This can be both an advantage and a disadvantage. If the asset is absolutely critical to the running of your business you could not afford to have it repossessed through the non-payment of the instalments. On the other hand, if you wind up your business on a voluntary basis it does give you the option of returning the item as no longer being required.

USING HIRE PURCHASE

Hire purchase is also sometimes referred to as lease purchase although it is not the same as leasing which is looked at separately in the next section. Hire purchase is probably the easiest and most flexible type of funding that you can obtain. You only need to walk down your local high street to see the range and extent of the schemes that are available and, it has to be pointed out, the widely differing range of costs involved.

Hire purchase agreements are usually very flexible, offering interest rates on variable or fixed terms. Repayment is usually scheduled to coincide with the working life of the asset and can range from 12 months to seven years.

Assessing features and benefits

Hire purchase is an agreement to purchase an asset, for example a motor vehicle, with defined repayments over an agreed term. Depending upon the actual terms and conditions of the agreement, ownership of the asset may or may not pass to you immediately. Some agreements, for obvious reasons, do not allow ownership of the asset to be transferred to you until all instalments have been paid.

In accounting terms, however, the asset is treated as being owned by you and it will appear in your balance sheet from the outset. The outstanding hire purchase will also appear as a debt in the liabilities section. The legislation regarding the tax allowances from the Inland Revenue and the reclaiming of VAT is subject to change each year and you should check for yourself the current situation. Your accountant will be able to give you specialist advice on this aspect of the finance.

Hire purchase can sometimes be cheaper than traditional bank finance. This is often the case where the manufacturer of the goods also provides the finance to enable a purchase to be made. As with all finance, however, you need to check the exact APR if you are to make realistic comparisons.

Assessing the disadvantages

The disadvantages of hire purchase are the same as if you had bought the item outright. If it breaks down, unless it is under guarantee, you will be responsible for the repairs despite the fact that ownership of the item is probably not vested in you. In addition, if for example you buy a motor vehicle on hire purchase you will be responsible for ongoing maintenance which in some circumstances, in order to protect the value of the asset, may be part of the terms and conditions of the finance.

You also need to check the terms and conditions carefully for any penalties which will be invoked if the agreement is broken. The hire purchase agreement is for a defined term and the finance company will have priced the cost of repayment based on the whole term. In some cases, the majority of repayments may be at a substantially reduced rate with a large final payment being required to actually purchase the asset outright.

The final disadvantage is also related to the ease with which hire purchase can be obtained. You need to be aware that some financing deals which may perhaps offer an 'interest free' period are actually quite expensive. After the relevant period, unless the finance is paid off in full, you could find yourself facing an interest rate that equates to in excess of 30% per annum. This is a lesson that you need to remember. Always be sure that you understand all the terms, conditions and costs of any form of finance before you sign on the dotted line.

CONSIDERING LEASING

As with hire purchase, leasing is an extremely flexible form of finance. A lease is negotiated with the lessor, i.e. the finance company, who acquires the asset that has been chosen by the lessee, i.e. you. The assets which can be leased are wide and varied. Photocopiers, computer systems, office furniture, motor vehicles, machine tools, and heavy plant and equipment are all examples.

Leasing should be distinguished from hiring. Hiring requires the user to select an item from stock already held by the hirer. Leasing enables the lessee to select any item from any manufacturer or supplier. The choice is therefore unlimited. The leasing agreement will be tailor-made for the actual asset involved.

Comparing different types of lease

There are three types of lease:

- finance lease
- operating lease
- contract hire.

Finance lease

With a finance lease the lessor pays for the asset and becomes the owner. The lessee then pays a rental which covers the capital cost of the asset together with interest and service charges. The purpose of this type of lease is solely to provide finance to the lessee on the security of the asset. The lessee is responsible for all maintenance and insurance.

Operating lease

Operating leases are mainly undertaken by manufacturers of

products that tend to be highly specialised or technical. The lease usually provides that the lessor is responsible for servicing, maintenance and updating of the equipment. Operating leases can also enable the lessee to avoid some of the risks of ownership, for example obsolescence.

Contract hire
Contract hire is similar to an operating lease. One of the most common uses of contract hire is to finance a fleet of motor vehicles. In this case the lessor takes responsibility for the regular maintenance and servicing of the vehicles. The lessee merely has to consider the day-to-day fuel costs.

Assessing the advantages
Leasing provides a number of advantages over other forms of finance:

- The lessor retains ownership of the asset and, using the asset as full security, a more competitive finance cost may be available.

- The lease is for a fixed term and, whilst the leasing payments are being made by the lessee, unlike bank facilities which are usually repayable on demand, the facility cannot be withdrawn.

- Apart from an initial advance monthly or quarterly payment, leasing does not involve any capital outlay.

- The lease can be flexible and in some cases the rental payments can be adjusted to take account of seasonal variations in trade.

- The income generated by using the asset in the business should make the costs of leasing self-financing.

- There may be tax advantages in that the whole costs of leasing can usually be offset against taxable income.

Assessing the disadvantages
There are also disadvantages to leasing:

- As a start-up business it can be very difficult to obtain lease finance.

- Leased assets cannot be used as security for any other type of funding – the asset is not yours.

- There may be restrictions on the use of the leased asset and the lessor may insist on approving your insurance arrangements.

- Because the asset is not yours you are not entitled to any residual value in the asset after it reaches the end of its working life.

- There is no entitlement to claim capital allowances for taxation purposes.

Taxation issues can play a large part in the decision whether or not to use leasing. You need to examine the financial, and indeed the non-financial, factors before you make any decision. Seek the advice of an accountant or a tax specialist to define the effects that lease finance options will have on your business.

GAINING A COMMERCIAL MORTGAGE

With the traditional differences between banks and building societies being eroded by a competitive market, more and more financing options are available. This is even more evident now that many of the historic differences between building societies and banks have been removed, with some of the building societies losing their mutuality and converting to banks. Among these is the long-term lending by building societies to commercial customers.

What is a commercial mortgage?
Commercial mortgages are, in effect, the same as the mortgages available to personal customers. They are, therefore, only generally available if you are considering the purchase of premises. In some circumstances, however, a commercial mortgage can be available for other business purposes but in all cases the loan will be secured on commercial property.

The individual terms and conditions of a commercial mortgage will vary from funder to funder, and the minimum loan amount will range from £100,000 to £250,000, although the maximum loan amount is normally unlimited. This will, of course, relate to the value of the security available.

Assessing the advantages

The principal advantage of a commercial mortgage over a bank loan for the same purpose is that the building society will often consider granting a greater percentage of the overall cost.

Traditionally a bank will offer anything between 45% and 70% of the total cost of the property. In addition, the value that the bank places on the property may be based on a forced sale basis rather than an open market valuation. These have already been explained in Chapter 5 but in simple terms the differences between the two are:

- Forced sale valuation – the price that the bank expects to achieve after all costs of sale and based on the principle that the property will be offered at a price to achieve a sale in the short-term.

- Open market valuation – the price that could be achieved in the market without undue time pressure on the sale being made. It is also calculated before the costs of the sale are deducted.

Building societies, on the other hand, are usually much more flexible. They will generally lend between 60% and 90% of the open market value, although in some cases they are prepared to finance 100% of the total cost of the property. Each proposition is taken on its merits.

Taking advantage of repayment flexibility

The repayments on a commercial mortgage can also sometimes be more flexible than for a bank loan. These can include repayment of the capital and interest on a monthly, quarterly, or even annual basis. The interest rate charged on a commercial mortgage can also be substantially lower than that charged by a bank. In some cases you could be able to negotiate an interest rate as low as 1% over base rate. In other cases the rate could be linked to the London Inter Bank Offer Rate (LIBOR) which can also be cheaper.

You will, however, need to check the terms of the mortgage as to when the interest is actually charged to the loan. This can affect the APR which may in true terms be substantially more than the interest rate quoted.

A further example of the flexibility of a commercial mortgage is where repayment of the capital sum is deferred until the end of the loan and interest only is repayable in the meantime. Referred to as bullet repayment terms, the loan can be repaid at the end of the term by a variety of means. These can include sale of the property, repayment from pension or life assurance proceeds, or any other secure method acceptable to the lender.

KEY POINTS

- Purchasing an asset gives you a number of alternative sources of finance – take time to check all your available options.

- Make sure you are clear on the differences between hire purchase and leasing and the way in which such finance is treated in your balance sheet.

- Always read all the terms and conditions of any agreement before you sign it – look for any penalty clauses.

- Check carefully the annual percentage rate (APR) that you are being charged – it can differ substantially from the interest rate quoted.

- Consider a commercial mortgage if the purchase of a large commercial property forms part of your plans – you can also consider this option if you are looking to re-finance your business and have sufficient security available.

7

Raising Funds from Within the Business

Many businesses are operated with such scant regard for looking after their finances that it is sometimes difficult to believe. The same applies to new businesses. If you plan your finances correctly you may find that you can reduce the external funding requirement. The aim of this chapter is to demonstrate how you can become more efficient in managing your working capital.

In the first part of this chapter we will look at options for gaining faster payment from your debtors. You have to recognise, however, that some of these schemes, for example factoring, may not be initially available to you. Having said that, if you understand how they operate and whether they could be beneficial to you, you can give them consideration later when your business has become established.

GAINING FASTER PAYMENT

The easiest way to gain faster payment for your business is not to allow credit to any of your customers. This might be fine in an ideal world but unfortunately it is more than likely that you will have to grant credit at some stage. When this happens it is vitally important that you do not allow your debtors undue time to pay you. You will have to pay your own creditors and it is therefore crucial that you keep tight control of your debtors.

If you are going to allow your customers time to pay you then make sure that your terms of trade are quite clear. If you are going to allow them 30 days to pay you then make sure they know that. The most common causes of late payment are due to unclear terms of trade. Always ensure that your invoices carry details of what time you will allow, and the penalties that could be charged in the absence of timely payment.

Failure to pay your creditors on time could also render you liable to penalties. The Late Payment of Commercial Debts Act 1998 was introduced to reduce the common abuse of credit facilities. The legislation was phased in over three years and it now allows all businesses to charge interest on outstanding invoices at the rate of 8% above Bank of England Base Rate. Where no credit terms have been agreed this interest can be charged after the invoice remains unpaid after 30 days.

Factoring your debts

A **factoring** service enables you to bridge the gap between sending the invoice and actually receiving payment. It is specifically designed for small businesses, usually with turnover of at least £250,000 although sometimes lower limits are available. The factor will take over the running of your sales ledger and will issue statements and debtor reminders according to an agreed timetable.

Factoring your debts means that you can obtain an immediate advance against your outstanding debtors. This usually equates to a maximum of 80% of approved invoices. In this case approved means that the customers have been approved as debtors by the factoring company. The factor also assumes control of your sales ledger, issuing statements and reminders on a set basis.

The advantages of factoring
- It improves cash flow with a faster collection of trade debts.

- It removes the need to chase unpaid invoices.

- It is a simple process and insurance against bad debts may be available.

The disadvantages of factoring
- Your customers know that you are using the factor – in some cases this does have a stigma attached to it.

- It can prove costly in overall terms.

- Once you have taken out a factoring arrangement it can be difficult to extricate yourself from it.

Invoice discounting

Invoice discounting operates on broadly the same principles as factoring but with two main differences:

- Control of the sales ledger is retained by you, and you will therefore need to control the debtors and chase for late payment yourself.

- Because you retain control, the existence of the invoice discounting arrangement is not evident to your customers – it is entirely confidential.

Because the principles are broadly the same in each case, both factoring and invoice discounting share the same advantages and disadvantages. The only difference, of course, is the perception of your customers when, rather than dealing with you concerning their invoices, they deal with the factor.

Selling your debts

The effects of selling your debts can be very wide ranging. I have already covered the fact that your customers might consider that there is some stigma attached to your business.

The major effect is that you will almost certainly be unable to gain a bank overdraft for working capital facilities. The reason for this is simple. By gaining payment from your debtors almost straight away this removes any requirement for further working capital. In effect you are gaining funding for your business before you actually need to pay your own creditors.

If you still find that you are having cash flow difficulties after arranging a factoring or invoice discount facility it is probably a sign that there are other fundamental problems within your business. I also cannot stress enough the inherent problems involved with actually ever repaying the factor or invoice discounter. Unless you can do this from your own resources by gradually reducing reliance on these facilities it is unlikely that you will ever be able to arrange alternative finance to pay them off.

Make sure that you consider both factoring and invoice discounting very carefully before you enter any agreement. Seek the assistance of your accountant or other advisor to investigate the exact implications on your business.

NEGOTIATING WITH CREDITORS

Many start-up businesses do not consider that they will be able to gain any credit from their suppliers. This is not always the case. **Trade credit** as it is known can be available but it will depend on the circumstances. If, for example, you are starting your business at an early age, having just left school or university, then you may have problems obtaining credit.

If, on the other hand, you have been employed for many years in the same industry that you are now starting your own business in you may find that obtaining trade credit is not difficult. You have an established track record in the industry and probably already know the suppliers with whom you will be dealing.

Gaining trade credit

The essential point is that you must research what is available. In other words, before you even start your business you must establish how much credit you can obtain and how long you will be given to pay. You cannot, for example, draw up any meaningful cash flow forecasts unless you assume from the outset that no credit will be available.

It can also take time to negotiate trade credit. In most cases some form of reference will be required, probably from your bank. All banks have different philosophies when it comes to giving a reference on their customers and you will need to check the exact position with your own bank.

Having gained agreement to a credit account it is extremely important that you do not abuse that facility. It can be as easily withdrawn as it was granted and this could place severe pressure on your cash flow. Always adhere to the agreed terms of the credit and make payment promptly when it is required.

Failure to pay on time could also render you liable to penalties. Remember that the provisions of the Late Payment of Commercial Debt Act mentioned earlier will also apply to debts that you owe. Bearing in mind the substantial statutory interest rate, the charges involved could represent a substantial amount and it is therefore something that you should avoid at all cost. If, of course, your creditors start to charge you on this basis it is also likely that they will have already withdrawn your credit facility.

Using credit cards
Another aspect of gaining credit that most business owners ignore is the fact that personal credit cards can also, at least initially, be used for this purpose. Most credit cards allow for up to 56 days' interest-free credit provided the outstanding balance is settled in full. There is absolutely nothing to stop you using this facility for your business although you will need to keep a careful track of the relevant records.

Trying different suppliers

Trade credit is not something that is only available to established businesses. In these times of intense competition suppliers need to be flexible in how they make their sales. Do not be put off by an initial refusal, try another supplier and you may get a different answer.

Obtaining discounts

If you are unable to gain any trade credit when you start your business you should not be afraid of asking for a discount from your potential suppliers. They are, of course, gaining cash payment from you which you might actually have to fund through a working capital overdraft. This will be costing you interest and accordingly be reducing your potential profit margin. If you can mitigate this loss through a discount then so much the better.

For some reason many business owners are very reticent about negotiating discounts, or indeed any other incentives that the supplier could be giving them. It seems to be the culture that the price quoted is the only price available.

I would recommend that any potential business owner visit at least one antique or other such trade fair. It can be a very enlightening experience. You can instantly recognise the dealers by the approach that they take when asking the price of an item from another dealer. By the same token the normal customer adopts an entirely different approach. Telling you the two differing methods in this book will not convince you that there is an entire cultural difference. You need to see it for yourself.

BEING MORE EFFICIENT

At the start of this chapter I touched upon the inherent failure of most small businesses to adequately look after their finances. Problems are only recognised when all of a sudden the wages cannot be paid on a Friday night. It is absolutely essential that you look after and control the cash that is flowing in and out of your business.

Managing cash

Cash is like the flow of blood through your veins. If the flow stops you will die. In the same way, if the flow of cash into your business ceases, your business will not survive. Long-term and short-term cash flow planning are essential components of your business planning activities. In many cases a cash flow forecast is prepared too late and for the wrong reason, usually at the request of the bank to assess your request to borrow money.

A cash flow forecast is used to forecast the cash that will flow into and out of your business. It is not concerned with anything other than cash and will therefore not indicate whether you are making profits or losses. It is a vital tool in controlling your business to ensure that **liquidity** is maintained.

Liquidity, in terms of actual cash, is essential to all businesses no matter what their size. Orders from customers are of no value whatsoever if you do not have the funds to manufacture the goods. In the same way, a warehouse full of stock will not pay the wages unless the goods can be sold and thereby converted into cash.

Understanding, and indeed controlling, how the cash flows through your business is one of the most important management issues that you must address. In simplistic terms, cash flows through your business as follows:

Initial cash invested

↓

Purchase goods ←

↓   ↑

Sell to customers ↑

↓   ↑

Receive cash → ↑

From this simple diagram you can see that if any part of the process is disrupted, for example late or non-payment by your customers, then you are likely to encounter a shortage of cash. Planning for such disruptions in cash flow will give you greater control over your financial stability and, in the long run, the whole viability of your business.

Controlling stock

Controlling your stock is very important when you are considering finance for your business. Holding too little stock could mean that you lose sales but holding too much stock means that you have less cash available for other purposes. This means that you have to raise unnecessary finance which then costs you more money in interest.

Controlling your stock levels is, therefore, an important part of your financing. When you establish your business, you may consider that initially you are going to require say £10,000 of stock. In itself that will not affect your financing decisions. Provided your estimate is correct, you will actually require that amount of stock. The important part comes when you sell some of that stock and then need to replace it. The question is raised as to how much more stock you need and when you should order it.

Buying in bulk
Some businesses make the mistake of ordering in bulk in order to obtain discounts. This means that at any one time they probably have more stock than they can sell within a reasonable time. The effect of the discount is subsequently eroded because more cash than necessary is being used to finance those stock levels. If you are borrowing money for such purposes, for example by way of bank overdraft, the interest is probably costing you more than you gain from the discount.

If, on the other hand, you ignore the offer of discounts and only purchase the stock that you can actually sell within a reasonable time, you reduce the cash requirement, and consequently the interest paid on the overdraft. In real terms this would probably mean that you are actually better off in terms of profit. You should also consider using a stock control system pioneered in Japan and referred to as **just in time**.

'Just in time' stock control system
As the name would suggest products are supplied 'just in time' to be used and the need for stock is minimised. Originally used primarily in the manufacturing sector it is also relevant to all other types of business. The one thing that is essential in this technique is that you have confidence in your supplier.

If you are a manufacturer, supplies of components would be available at short notice or 'just in time' to be used in the manufacturing process. The same would apply if you are a wholesaler or retailer. Products would be supplied just before they are needed for sale.

In theoretical terms, as a retailer for example, this would mean that you need only carry sufficient stocks to fill your shelves. As sales were made these would be totalled up and orders placed for further supplies at the end of each day. The replacement products could then be delivered early the next day to be stocked on the shelves ready for sale.

In real terms, however, you would still need to plan for contingencies, for example the breakdown of the delivery van. It would still mean that your volume of stocks could be reduced. Rather than holding a supply of products that represent sales for one week, you may be able to reduce that down to two or three days' worth of stock.

KEY POINTS

- Keep tight control of your debtors and make sure that they actually pay you when the payment becomes due. Do not allow any late-payers because they will affect your ability to pay your own creditors.

- If you consider factoring or invoice discounting, consider carefully what this will mean – both can be difficult to ever repay and they can be expensive.

- Obtaining trade credit is not impossible for a start-up business – there are likely to be many sources for your supplies, so shop around.

- Never abuse your credit facilities – always pay your debts on time and you will establish a good track record for your business.

- Do not forget that you can use personal credit cards to obtain interest free credit – just make sure you keep accurate records.

- Keep tight control over your cash situation – make sure that you manage the flow of cash through your business properly.

- Examine your stock levels on a regular basis – cash tied up in stock cannot be used for other purposes.

8

Obtaining Grants and Other Assistance

There is a substantial amount of assistance available to small businesses. Unfortunately a great deal of this help is missed purely because of ignorance of the actual scheme. Some people do not seem to wish to discuss their plans to establish a new business and accordingly they can never receive appropriate help and advice.

The number of schemes available across the UK are wide and diverse, and offer both financial and non-financial assistance. It would be impossible to cover all the forms of assistance available and it will be up to you to find out what is available in your locality. What I can do is outline some of the types of assistance that are available to businesses in my own location, the North East of England.

APPLYING FOR GRANTS

The overriding principle for obtaining grants and other forms of financial assistance is that you must make your application, and have the assistance agreed, before you start your business. Unfortunately a lot of businesses miss out because they do not follow this simple rule.

There is a substantial amount of help available to new businesses in both a financial and non-financial form. It is absolutely essential that you research the position thoroughly. Some grants are reliant upon either jobs being created or investment in new plant and machinery. Others have no restrictions whatsoever and are available purely by making a simple application.

Local government assistance

Most local authorities offer a range of incentives and grants for businesses to create jobs in their area. Some new businesses overlook this source of funding on the basis that they are creating no new jobs. This is factually incorrect. If you are starting your own business you are, at the very least, creating a new job for yourself.

You should contact the Economic Development Office within your local authority to find out what you may be eligible for because there will be some diversity across the UK. To give you some specific examples, however, the following schemes are available from the City of Sunderland Council:

- **Rent relief grants** – available for between 25% and 50% of the rent payable for the first year of a new lease.

- **Basic services grants** – a 50% grant is available for the provision of new and essential services including electricity, gas or drainage work.

- **Interest relief grant** – amounting to 5% per annum for up to two years of the value of loans used to purchase machinery or buildings for industrial use.

- **Removal grants** – available to cover up to 50% of eligible costs incurred to move to industrial premises in the city.

- **Trainee employment grants** – grants are awarded to cover 75% of wages of new trainees in the first year and 25% in the second year.

- **Exhibition grants** – to cover 50% of the costs of exhibiting at a recognised trade exhibition outside the North East up to a maximum of £5,000.

For obvious reasons all these grants have eligibility criteria in addition to which they are entirely discretionary. This means that even if you do qualify you may still not receive the funding because the Council may not have any money left for the scheme.

Central government assistance
The Small Business Service was established to help businesses and to represent their interests across government. It works closely with the network of Business Links in England, Business Shops in Scotland, Business Connect in Wales, and Ednet in Northern Ireland. These centres should be your first port of call if you are thinking of starting a business and we will look at the assistance they can provide later in this chapter.

Through the Small Business Service, the government offers a

number of schemes which can provide assistance in terms of either grants or awards. The three main schemes are:

- Regional Selective Assistance (RSA)
- Regional Enterprise Grant (REG)
- Small Firms Merit Award for Research and Technology (SMART).

Regional Selective Assistance
RSA is a discretionary scheme aimed at attracting investment and creating or safeguarding jobs in selected areas of the UK. Grants are available for qualifying projects with total project expenditure in excess of £500,000 and can range from 5% to 15% of the fixed project costs. Each application is individually assessed, and the actual amount of the grant will depend on the area, the project and the number of jobs involved.

Regional Enterprise Grant
REG is also available only in selected areas of the UK and there are variations in the eligibility criteria depending on location. The grant is available up to a maximum of £75,000 on projects which involve up to £500,000 of capital investment. In general, high growth businesses seeking to maximise value added projects with quality output are given a preference (see Figure 7).

SMART
Previously an annual award granted on a competitive basis, the SMART scheme is now available on a grant basis. Grants can be claimed by small and medium-sized businesses to help make better use of technology, and to develop technologically innovative products and processes (see Figure 8). There are six different types of grants available under the scheme:

- **Technology reviews** – up to £2,500 towards the costs of expert reviews against best practice.

- **Technology studies** – up to £5,000 to help identify technological opportunities leading to innovative products and processes.

- **Micro projects** – up to £10,000 to help develop low-cost prototypes of products and processes involving technical advances and/or novelty.

Application for an Enterprise Grant for an Investment Project

• Please type your answers or write in black ink
• Use N/A for 'Not Applicable'

Please note: Your business can only receive one Enterprise Grant
Important: do not start your project until a formal decision is given

Applicant Details

1 Name of applicant

2a Correspondence address
(please give Local Authority ward if known)

Address

County   Post Code

Local Authority ward

2b If the Government Office needs to discuss your application whom should they contact

Name

Telephone No   Fax No

3 Where is the project to take place if different from above address
(please include Local Authority ward if known)

Address

County   Post Code

Local Authority ward

4 Applicant's business status
(please tick correct box; if a limited company give your company registration number)

☐ Non Quoted Limited Company   Registration No

☐ Partnership

☐ Other   Specify

Fig. 7. Extract from an application form for Regional Enterprise Grant.

Smart
Application Form
Feasibility Studies and Development Projects

* Please read the Guidance Notes carefully before you complete this form.
* Please type your answers, or write in black ink using BLOCK LETTERS. This form is available electronically at www.BusinessAdviceOnline.org/smart
* To apply you must complete the application form and provide a detailed Project Proposal, as set out in the Guidance Notes.
* Where boxes are provided please mark the correct box with a tick.
* We will publish information from Questions 1-17 of this form if you receive an award.

Applicant Details

Smart
Funding Innovation

1. In what capacity are you applying? (Individual, sole trader/proprietor, partnership or company)

2. Your business name or your name (if an individual/sole trader) or the name of the proprietor or a partner (if a partnership).

3. Your business address

Postcode

Website

4. Who should we contact to discuss your application?

Name

Position in organisation

Telephone number   Fax

e-mail

Fig. 8. Extract from an application form for SMART scheme.

- **Feasibility studies** – up to £45,000 towards undertaking feasibility studies into innovative technologies.

- **Development projects** – up to £150,000 towards undertaking development projects.

- **Exceptional development projects** – up to £450,000 for a small number of exceptional high-cost development projects.

Guidance notes and eligibility criteria for all three of the schemes above are available free of charge from the Department of Trade and Industry (Dti).

European assistance
Grants may be available from the European Union through the European Structural Funds. These include:

- European Regional Development Fund (ERDF)
- European Social Fund (ESF).

The criteria for obtaining such grants is decided by the members of the European Union and the actual amount available, and indeed the member states which can benefit, are subject to constant review. At the time of writing the UK will receive over £10 billion for regeneration and economic development for the years 2000 to 2006.

The Dti co-ordinates the administration of the available funds throughout the UK in conjunction with the Scottish, Welsh and Northern Ireland Offices and in England through the Local Government Offices. These grants are extremely complicated and if you consider that you may be eligible you need to seek specialist advice. Early contact with your Local Government Office is essential because grants from the European Union are sometimes only considered by committees which meet once a year.

KNOWING THE DIFFICULTIES

With the exception of the grants and assistance available from your local authority which are relatively straightforward, you need to consider carefully whether the time and effort that you will put into making a grant application is actually worthwhile.

The process can be extremely long and drawn out and you can be sure that you will face a number of hurdles on the way. A word of warning at this stage. If you are approached by a company which states that they can help you identify and obtain grants in return for an up-front fee you need to be very wary. A number of such scam operations have been seen in the past where businesses have lost a considerable amount of money.

Advice on obtaining grants is freely available through the network of Business Links and other support organisations. In some locations there is actually someone from the Dti within the offices of the Business Link with whom you can informally discuss your plans to see what may be available. There is absolutely no need for you to pay anyone for information on the grants or other assistance that may be available.

Meeting the criteria

Invariably there are very strict criteria involved for actually receiving a grant. You must understand exactly what is involved before you make an application. Some grants only involve capital expenditure on fixed assets and others will allow the full project costs, including any working capital element, to be included in the calculations.

Always read carefully the literature that comes with the application forms. This will tell you how and when the application should be made, what supporting documentation will be required, for example a full business plan and financial projections for three years, and give clear guidelines on the amount that can be claimed.

Completing the application

Some application forms for grants are extremely complicated, especially those from central government and the European Union. It is vitally important that the application is completed correctly. In addition, you must remember that most grants are only available as 'gap' funding, i.e. the finance cannot be obtained elsewhere and the project cannot be completed without the grant.

Unfortunately a lot of businesses consider that if they are investing money they should be eligible for a grant. That may have been the case some years ago but policy guidelines have changed. You must demonstrate the actual need for the grant. Even if you do qualify you must again remember that most grants are discretionary.

I would recommend to you most strongly that if you are applying for a grant you should seek professional help with completing the application. Advisors within Business Links and the other support organisations are well versed in the procedures involved. They can help you to ensure that your application is made as attractive and realistic as possible.

Waiting for the answer

Having made your application you will be in a state of limbo. Under normal circumstances most projects cannot be commenced until the grant application has been approved. This means that you cannot do anything, or spend any money, on the project at all.

Following receipt of your application the grant provider is likely to want to visit you and discuss your proposals further. This process will be similar to that undertaken by conventional funders and you need to be absolutely prepared. At this stage you might like to review the content and advice given in Chapter 3 because the same considerations will apply.

The actual time-scale following receipt of your application and receiving an answer can vary considerably. In many cases the time taken is in direct proportion to the amount of grant that you are seeking. Remember that you are often dealing with bureaucracy and accordingly you should be prepared for a long wait.

Expecting cuts and conditions

You also need to understand that your application for a grant may be scaled down. In other words, you may not receive the amount of grant that you have requested. You can be certain that your application will be scrutinised thoroughly and if the grant provider considers that cost savings can be made in any area of your application they will insist upon them. When, and if, you get a positive response to your grant application it may also be subject to a number of terms and conditions.

Actually getting the money

On the assumption that your grant application has been successful, actually getting the money can also be a long and drawn-out process. In many cases the money may need to be spent first and receipts provided before the grant can be obtained. This in itself can be a major hurdle to overcome especially where the grant is for a substantial sum.

Where other terms and condition have been imposed, for example job creation, you may also need to prove that such jobs have been created before the grant will be paid. The number of terms and conditions will vary on an individual basis. What you need to ensure is that they are fulfilled as quickly as possible to enable you to make a claim for the grant.

At this stage you can see why I have given the advice that you need to think carefully about making an application for a grant. It is not an easy process and it can involve some pain on the way. In addition, many grants are taxable and the benefits can therefore be substantially reduced.

LOOKING FOR LOCAL HELP

There is a large range of organisations that offer help and advice to their members on running a business, for example, the Forum of Private Business and the Small Business Federation. Details of these and other organisations are in the Useful Contacts section at the end of this book.

Business support organisations

As mentioned previously, the best places to gain advice and guidance on running a business are through the Business Links in England, Business Shops in Scotland, Business Connect in Wales, and Ednet in Northern Ireland. Quite apart from the advice and guidance that they offer, they can also provide financial and non-financial grants to your business.

Financial grants from these business support organisations have, however, been substantially reduced in recent years and are only generally available in small amounts, somewhere between £100 to £250. The main provision of assistance comes in a non-financial form. Examples include help with:

- design and production of business cards and stationery
- advice on putting together your business plan
- guidance on market research and strategy for your proposed business.

Some of these take the form of training courses and others, for example design work, are undertaken by experienced professionals employed on a consultancy basis. In most cases all this support is offered free of charge.

Support is also available through these organisations on a subsidised basis where accredited consultants are employed to assist you and their fee is only partly payable by you. As an example, in Sunderland a 50% grant of up to £2,000 is available towards the costs of employing a professional to design your website. However, the support that will be available does vary widely and you must approach your local advice centre yourself.

The British Chambers of Commerce

The Member Chambers of the British Chambers of Commerce (BCC) are subject to tough accreditation criteria to ensure that they offer the very best in business support. Membership of an individual Chamber can, however, be expensive and the actual cost is defined by the size of your business. The BCC do offer a number of services to members quite apart from campaigning on behalf of members in both local and central government concerns.

Information and events
Information and advice on all aspects of running a business is available, in addition to which the individual Chambers organise a number of networking events and conferences each year.

Training
Collectively the British Chambers of Commerce are the largest single provider in the UK, delivering in excess of 7,500 courses each year for over 110,000 people from businesses of all sizes.

Export assistance
The individual Chambers operate schemes to assist with export opportunities, and can offer assistance with arranging attendance at trade missions and fairs throughout the world.

Cost savings
Taking advantage of its bulk purchasing power the BCC negotiates exclusive deals with national suppliers to offer members generous savings on high quality business services.

The Prince's Trust

If you are looking to start your own business, and are between 18 and 30 years of age and presently unemployed, you may be able to receive assistance from The Prince's Trust. This assistance can take a number of different forms including:

- a low-interest loan of up to £5,000
- test-marketing grants of up to £250
- grants of up to £1,500 in special circumstances
- advice from an appointed 'business mentor' during the first three years
- extra support including discounted exhibition space and specialist advice.

The Prince's Trust operates through a number of area offices throughout the UK. To qualify for help you need to have a viable business idea and have been refused all or some of the finance from any other source.

Shell *live*WIRE

If you are between 16 and 30 years of age you can gain assistance from Shell *live*WIRE which is an investment programme funded by Shell UK. They can offer you help with starting a business and provide factsheets, if available, on your business idea.

A number of different schemes are available, including an annual award competition which provides both a financial reward and other non-financial assistance in your first 18 months of trading. The competition is run on a local, regional, and national basis and can provide a great deal of publicity.

There are over 100 offices throughout the country and you should contact the national co-ordinator for a free booklet which outlines all the schemes in greater detail.

KEY POINTS

- Find out what assistance may be available before you start your business – do not miss out purely through ignorance.

- Discuss your business proposals with an advisor from your local Business Link or other support organisation – their advice is free so take advantage of it.

- Consider carefully whether the time and effort necessary to apply for a grant is actually worthwhile – gaining some grants can be a lengthy and complex process.

- Never pay anyone who claims that they can research and obtain a grant on your behalf in exchange for a fee – you will more than likely lose your money.

9

Seeking Specialist Funding

There are a large number of specialist lending schemes throughout the UK and it would be impossible to give you details of every single one. You will need to make your own enquiries, probably with the assistance of your local Business Link. In this chapter we will, therefore, look at some of the types of specialist schemes that may be appropriate for your business.

GAINING AN EQUITY PARTNER

Most small businesses avoid **equity** at all costs on the basis that they want to maintain sole control. For most small business start-ups they will not actually be able to gain equity funding, even if they wanted it, because providers of such capital are usually only interested in making a substantial investment. The normal criteria for most venture capitalists is a minimum equity investment of £250,000.

In some circumstances, however, especially where your own capital contribution is small and your borrowing requirement is large, equity funding will be essential as part of the overall package of funding. We have, of course, already looked at the gearing aspect in Chapter 1.

For the start-up business there are two likely sources of equity funding:

- Business Angels
- venture capital.

Business Angels

Business Angels are high net worth individuals with a background of running their own successful business. Their motivation for investing in small businesses, quite apart from the financial gain they hope to make, is actually for the fun and enjoyment of being involved with a particular business. For this reason they are highly selective in the investments that they make. It is estimated that only perhaps one in ten applications will actually succeed in gaining funding.

Quite apart from considering that you have a sound proposal they will also take a very 'hands on' approach in the running of your business. This can be both an opportunity and a burden to you. You will be able to take advantage of their business expertise and acumen, but they will expect to be involved in all decisions made concerning the business.

Most Business Angels will only invest in businesses located in close proximity to where they live. You may find that your local Business Link will have their own register of potential Business Angels, but even if they do not they can point you in the right direction. As an alternative you can use the services of the National Business Angels Network.

National Business Angels Network (NBAN)
NBAN is a service that works across the UK to achieve introductions between Business Angels and businesses seeking finance. It is sponsored by the major high street banks and a number of other experienced professional firms. NBAN provides an efficient low cost service, sourcing risk capital for small and medium-sized businesses which is provided by private investors in return for shares in the business.

Businesses seeking finance complete an application form (see Figure 9), detailing their funding requirements, which is reviewed by the NBAN head office in London. Once accepted by NBAN, brief details are then circulated to potential Business Angels via the NBAN website and through the monthly publication. At this stage the identity of the business is not revealed, it is entirely confidential.

If a potential registered Business Angel is interested in the business they can then access further details which are password protected on the website, and request a copy of the full business plan. Businesses also have the opportunity to make presentations at an NBAN local meeting, in addition to which they are given the option to access other investor networks.

Venture capital
Venture capital firms will only accept businesses with high growth potential and which are managed by skilled, ambitious owners. There are a number of defined stages in the development of a business where venture capital could be considered.

Business registration form

National
Business Angels
Network

company name

Contact details

title   last name   first name   position

address

post code

telephone (day)   (mobile)

fax   e-mail

Nature of business describe the business sector you operate in

Stage of business development

pre-start up ☐	development/expansion	☐
start up/innovation ☐	sale/MBO/MBI	☐
early stage ☐		

How did you hear about National Business Angels Network?

organisation

Intermediary do you have an adviser who has agreed to handle enquiries from prospective investors?

☐ yes   ☐ no

if yes give details

organisation

contact name

address

post code

telephone   fax   e-mail

if no, you will be referred to your local National Business Angels Network Agent

Bank details

name

town

Business plan

is there a business plan available?   ☐ yes   ☐ no   ☐ in preparation

if yes, was the plan produced by

yourself   ☐ yes   ☐ no

adviser   ☐ yes   ☐ no

if yes, adviser name

Financial information provide information on historic and/or projected trading (all figures in £000s)

	full year before last	last full year	current period to date	current full year forecast	next full year forecast
number of months in period					
period end (month)					
turnover	£	£	£	£	£
profit before tax	£	£	£	£	£
net worth/shareholders funds		£	£		
total borrowings		£	£		
cash/liquid investments		£	£		
audited accounts	☐ yes ☐ no	☐ yes ☐ no			

continued overleaf

Fig. 9. National Business Angels Network registration form.

Enterprise Investment Scheme for further information contact your local tax office

does your business comply? ☐ yes ☐ no ☐ don't know

Marketing literature

does your business have brochures available? ☐ yes ☐ no

Investment required give a breakdown of the total amount of investment required (£000s)

purchase of assets	£
purchase of shares	£
repayment of borrowings	£
research and development	£
product launch/marketing	£
additional working capital	£
other	£
total required	**£**

Investment sources indicate how the total specified above will be financed (£000s)

shareholders/promoters	£	
bank	£	
other borrowings	£	
investors already identified	£	
required from new investor(s)	**£**	this figure will feature in the monthly publication and on the website
total		

Equity available indicate what share of the equity you are prepared to offer the investor

☐ up to 25% ☐ up to 50% ☐ negotiable

Investor skills input state the most useful business skills and management expertise that an investor could bring to your business

☐ general management ☐ finance ☐ marketing/sales ☐ production ☐ HR/administration

Investor involvement indicate the involvement you require or are prepared to offer an investor

☐ less than 2 days a month ☐ 3-10 days a month ☐ over 10 days a month

Exit route indicate your aspirations for realising your own and that of your investors' interests

your exit timeframe	☐ 1-2 years	☐ 3-4 years	☐ 5-7 years	☐ 8+ years	☐ no plans
likely route	☐ trade sale	☐ float	☐ MBO	☐ MBI	☐ other
investor's exit timeframe	☐ 1-2 years	☐ 3-4 years	☐ 5-7 years	☐ 8+ years	☐ no plans
likely route	☐ trade sale	☐ float	☐ MBO	☐ MBI	☐ other

I hereby confirm that the company agrees to subscribe to the National Business Angels Network Limited in accordance with the conditions set out overleaf and to comply with the obligations contained in these conditions.

signed _____ position _____ date _____
for and on behalf of the company

Please send the completed form and your cheque for £150 + VAT (£176.25) made out to National Business Angels Network Limited to:

Alternatively, please send us your credit card number and expiry date. Regrettably, we are unable to take American Express.

National Business Angels Network
40-42 Cannon Street
London EC4N 6JJ

Tel 020 7329 2929
Fax 020 7329 2626
e-mail info@bestmatch.co.uk
website www.bestmatch.co.uk

Seed capital
Seed capital has already been considered in Chapter 2. You need to be aware that very few seed capital investments are made each year by venture capitalists. They are usually made in businesses with a new high-technology product that will provide real innovation, and accordingly high returns.

Start-up capital
Although most start-up businesses are typically small in size, there is an increasing number of multi-million pound businesses being started. This has been evidenced by the revolution caused by the Internet and the subsequent increase in the number of dot com businesses being started. With the recent number of such business failures, however, the venture capital funders will be more reticent about making such investments.

Expansion capital
This is by far the largest single use of venture capital, accounting for over 50% of such investments. Funding is generally made available to finance increased production capacity, product development, marketing, and to provide additional working capital.

Finding a venture capitalist
All of the venture capitalists in the UK are represented by the British Venture Capital Association (BVCA). The BVCA publishes an annual directory of members which is available free of charge. The directory lists venture capital firms as well as their investment preferences and full contact details. It also provides details of a wealth of other organisations and professionals that are experienced in the venture capital field.

How will the investment be made?
In most cases the investment by the venture capitalist will be made by way of share-holding. The actual structure of the share capital that will be used will depend upon the requirements of the investor. It is normal, however, for the investment to take the form of **preference shares**.

Preference shares rank ahead of all other types of share for both income and repayment of capital. Their income rights are defined and they are usually entitled to a fixed rate of dividend payment. The shares may also be redeemable only on fixed dates and sometimes at a fixed premium. Only in exceptional circumstances will the preference shares be expressed as irredeemable. If this is the case, you need to exercise extreme caution. Your entire right to buy back the shares has been taken away and you are, in effect, unable to ever repay the investment.

How much will venture capital cost?
A venture capitalist will usually look to retain their investment for between three and seven years. The exact way in which the investment will be redeemed will be tailored to suit each individual business. You can, however, expect the venture capitalist to be looking for an annual return of probably at least 30% and in some cases substantially more. The rate of return is directly proportional to the perceived risk. The normal ways in which venture capital is redeemed include:

- Selling the shares back to the company.
- Selling the shares to another investor, perhaps another venture capitalist.
- A trade sale where the whole business is sold to another.
- The business achieves its own stockmarket listing.

As with all forms of funding you need to understand the exact terms and conditions on which it is being made available. If you are looking for equity finance in any form you will need to seek specialist advice.

PROCURING SOFT LOANS

Soft loans are loans that are available on generous terms and at lower interest rates than would be charged commercially. In general terms they are provided through local Enterprise Agencies and are available where conventional funding, for example through a bank, cannot be obtained for any reason.

Enterprise Agencies are not-for-profit organisations which provide a wide variety of services to small businesses on a localised basis. The loan funds that they operate will be available on various terms and conditions and, in some circumstances, they are only available to people within a certain age band.

There are also a large number of organisations which provide soft loans, the funding for which is provided by large corporations. One example of such a fund is the loan fund operated through Northern

Enterprise in Newcastle-upon-Tyne which is sponsored by the Northern Rock. A further scheme, specifically designed for young entrepreneurs, is operated by the Prince's Youth Business Trust. In a similar manner the Royal British Legion operates a fund which is only available to ex-servicemen or women.

In some circumstances the provision of a soft loan can actually lead to further conventional funding being raised. The reason for this is that most soft loan fund managers take a personal interest in the businesses in which they invest, and accordingly they provide a high level of support and advice. This involvement can give confidence to the traditional funders, e.g. a bank manager, who know that a strict degree of control will be exercised.

This phenomenon is known as **leverage**. The soft loan levers further funding and reduces the risks for both funders. In some cases there are actually informal agreements between the managers who administer the soft loans funds and the high street banks. This works on the basis that the bank will match the amount of the loan that is made by the soft loan provider, usually up to an agreed maximum, in order that total funding for a project can be achieved on a shared basis.

The Phoenix Fund

The Phoenix Fund was introduced in 1999 and was designed specifically to encourage entrepreneurship in disadvantaged areas of the UK. It comprises four specific elements:

- the Development Fund
- Business Volunteer Mentoring Association
- Community Finance Initiatives (CFI)
- a Loan Guarantee Scheme.

The third of these, CFI, is operated by locally run, not-for-profit organisations that lend smaller amounts to businesses that cannot otherwise gain funding. The businesses must, however, be able to demonstrate that they will be self-sustainable and viable.

The CFI operates in clearly defined, deprived geographic areas and aims to support sections of the community which are socially excluded. In addition to providing support for traditional businesses the CFI will also support businesses that are run with a purely social objective, rather than for the sake of earning profits to be distributed to shareholders.

FUNDING RESEARCH AND DEVELOPMENT

Ongoing research and development plays a vital role for many businesses. It can also be the source of a great deal of speculative expenditure. For this reason the Dti operates a number of schemes to support businesses in the UK. In addition, in order to foster relations between businesses throughout the European Union, there is a specialist scheme that aims to encourage strategic alliances.

LINK

LINK is the government's principal mechanism for supporting collaborative research partnerships between industry and the sources of research. It provides financial support to individual programmes of research. LINK also aims to enhance the competitiveness of industry and the quality of people's lives through two main methods:

- Support for managed programmes of pre-competitive science and technology in market or technology sectors.

- Encouraging industry to invest in further work leading to commercially successful products, processes, systems and services.

Various government departments and research councils sponsor LINK programmes covering a wide range of technology, from food and bio-sciences to electronics and communication. Each programme supports a number of collaborative research projects, each normally lasting around two to three years.

Government funding provides up to 50% of eligible costs for each LINK project. The exact level of funding for each partner depends upon the allocation of work in the project. LINK funding is available on a programme by programme basis and further information can be obtained from the LINK Directorate.

EUREKA

EUREKA is a Europe-wide network for industrial research and development. Launched in 1985, it provides a framework through which industry and research institutes from the European Union develop and exploit the technologies crucial to global competitiveness and a better quality of life.
EUREKA offers:

- Help in finding partners from industry and research.
- Improved access to national public financing.
- Support and help in defining collaborative contracts between partners across the European Union.
- Involvement in European standardisation activities.
- Facilitated access to private funding sources.
- The EUREKA 'Label of Excellence'.

At least two different organisations in two different countries must participate in a EUREKA project. Co-operating with research institutes and businesses in other European countries can provide you with:

- more ideas
- complementary technical expertise and lower cost
- sharing the risks involved
- access to new and/or larger markets.

OBTAINING HELP WITH EXPORTING

If you are considering exporting you will need to gain specialist assistance. All the major high street banks have export departments that can help you explore the possibilities available. A further source of assistance is the British Chamber of Commerce. Your major source of assistance, however, will probably be through the Dti and Trade Partners UK.

Trade Partners UK provides a number of schemes, most of which are free to businesses. These include:

- The advice of an export development counsellor for initial planning advice and information on sources of help.

- Access to an export promoter for specialist advice on approaching a particular market.

- Tailored market research, at a nominal cost, undertaken by commercial staff based in overseas embassies.

The embassy staff can report on market conditions, opportunities, buyers, and potential partners and can help in arranging local visit programmes including the provision of an interpreter if necessary. In terms of the financial help available, Trade Partners UK provides:

- trade mission sponsorship
- exhibition and trade fair sponsorship
- a grant of up to 50% of your export market research costs.

Export Awards

The Export Awards for Small Businesses were established in 1969 to provide an annual showcase of best exporting practice and to encourage more small businesses to consider trading abroad. The awards are open to businesses with no more than 250 employees which can demonstrate a growth in export earnings over the past three years. In addition, the business must have made export sales of more than £100,000.

Awards are made to the winners from each of the 12 UK government office regions. Each regional winner receives £1,000 from Grant Thornton to be spent on an Exporting Benchmarking Consultation or Tax Sweep, one Komposs International edition, an interactive export toolkit from British Trade International and a further £500 to be used for the benefit of all employees.

In addition, the prizes won by the regional winners of the Best Newcomer will receive £2,000 from HSBC Trade Services. This can be spent on either the acquisition of further export skills, or investigating and developing new export markets. An overall winner of the regional awards receives further export services and prizes worth in excess of £7,500.

KEY POINTS

- Do not be afraid of seeking an equity partner – it is better to have a 60% share in a thriving business than a 100% share in a business that is under-capitalised.

- A Business Angel or venture capitalist will bring added experience to help you manage your business more successfully.

- Soft loans can often help 'lever' further funds – check with your local Business Link to see what funds may be available.

- If research and development within your business is going to be significant you should consider a strategic partnership through the Dti LINK scheme or EUREKA.

- Exporting for the first time carries a large degree of risk – make sure that you obtain specialist advice before you start.

10

Keeping Things Under Control

Once you have gained the funding for your business proposal there are a number of things that you need to do to ensure ongoing success. First you need to review the marketing side of your business to maintain your competitive advantage. Next you need to constantly update your financial projections to make sure that your actual performance is meeting your targets. Finally you need to keep tight control of your cash position.

REVIEWING THE MARKET

The importance of maintaining your unique selling point and competitive advantage, through ongoing market intelligence and competitor information, is vital. Up-to-date information about your market will keep you aware of changes or developments that could affect your business. This information may also indicate trends in consumer demand that you can exploit. It could also potentially help you to identify economic trends in the market that could affect the buying habits of your customers.

Keeping your eye on the ball

Market intelligence will enable you to update your sales forecasts on a regular basis and this will also assist you when reviewing your overall strategy. It is also critical that you keep track of your competitors. On a continuing basis you need to find out what they are doing, what they are charging and any new products they have launched which could compete with yours.

If you employ sales staff ensure that they obtain feedback from your customers. It is highly likely that your customers will also be looking at the activities of your competitors and it may be that they can provide you with 'inside' information. For example, it is not unknown for a competitor to approach a customer of a rival firm and offer some form of inducement such as a discount or better credit terms in order to gain their business. Unless you have information on this sort of activity at an early stage you could well find your customer base declining.

Staying competitive
Competitive advantage is everything in business. You must retain a unique selling point that will consistently bring you new customers as well as repeat business. The only way you can do this is to continually research the market in order to establish exactly what is happening.

Information is power and unless you have that power you may miss out on new opportunities available to you in the market. Even worse, you could succumb to new threats in the market that could destroy your business. You must take all necessary action to ensure that you stay ahead of the competition.

COMPARING ACTUAL AGAINST FORECAST PERFORMANCE

As part of their agreement to fund your business, some lenders may insist upon the production of regular, updated financial information. Even if they do not, if you are astute you will recognise that this is something you should have in any event. You need to keep track of your ongoing performance in order to ensure that your overall targets will be met.

The way to succeed in business is to constantly review and amend your business plan in the light of actual, as opposed to budgeted, performance. The process of business planning is a continuous cycle and does not stop with the construction of a business plan.

There is very little point in setting goals and objectives within your business plan unless you monitor how you are performing on an ongoing basis. This aspect is just as important as establishing the goals and objectives in the first place. Unfortunately, most entrepreneurs do not undertake this aspect of the planning process and only react after a problem has been encountered. If they had taken the time and trouble to monitor their business on a regular basis they may have been able to avoid the problem in the first place.

Keeping management accounts
Most new businesses totally ignore this aspect of running their business. Financial forecasts are put together, the business plan is

written and used to raise finance, and then the forecasts, along with the business plan, are put in a drawer and forgotten.

This can only be a recipe for disaster. Unless you carefully monitor your performance on a regular basis by compiling management accounts you run the risk of running out of cash and/or not making any profit. Once that happens it can be difficult to raise more finance because all you have demonstrated to the potential funder is that you have failed to keep control of your business.

On at least a monthly basis you should take some time to analyse your financial performance for that month. This means that you must categorise and total all your income and expenditure and compare the actual figures to your forecasted target figures. Ideally this should be done on a rolling cumulative basis in order that you can compare not only the monthly figures but also the cumulative figures to date.

Comparing your actual performance against your forecasted figures in this way will enable you to gain a greater understanding of exactly how your business is performing over time. It may well be that one month's figures could be distorted in some way, for example a large amount of capital expenditure being deferred for payment one month later than anticipated. This sort of distortion in the figures will have a large effect in both the forecasted month for the expenditure and the actual month in which it was incurred. By comparing the figures on a cumulative basis, however, this type of situation can be balanced out.

CONTROLLING THE FLOW OF CASH

In Chapter 7 it was emphasised that cash is like the flow of blood through your body. If there is any disruption to the flow of cash it will create serious problems for your business. It is absolutely essential that you undertake both long-term and short-term cash flow planning as part of your business management activities.

Profits do not mean cash

Just because a business shows a profit in the profit and loss account does not mean that such profit is actually held in cash although it has funded the business. It is more than likely that the cash generated from sales, including the profit element, has already been reinvested into the business. Such investment may be in current assets such as stock, which can be used to generate further cash, or fixed assets such as equipment which, of course, will not generate any cash return unless the asset is sold.

In both cases cash has been used to purchase an asset, effectively exchanging one asset for another, and accordingly the overall financial resources of the business have not changed. The funds remain in the business but the actual hard cash itself has been utilised. The profit shown in the accounts is therefore merely a book-keeping entry and does not mean that such a sum is sitting in a deposit account somewhere ready to be utilised.

Updating the cash flow forecasts
In the first chapter we looked at the use of cash flow forecasts as part of putting your funding proposal together. Over time, however, your forecasts will become obsolete and, as already stated earlier in this chapter, the forecasted figures can be replaced by actual figures to compile your management accounts.

By using this factual information you should then go one stage further and redraft your cash flow forecasts on a rolling basis. In this way you can quickly see if problems are likely to occur in the future which may require further funding.

Using source and application of funds statements
Funding for your business may also come from other sources that do not involve cash, for example creditors that allow you time to pay for your supplies. In the same way, you may also provide funds to your customers by allowing them time to pay you for goods they have received from you. Neither of these examples would involve any exchange of cash until either your customers pay for the goods or you pay your creditors.

Cash is a source of funds, but not all funds are cash. It is important that you understand the distinction so as to ensure that adequate liquid funds are available to finance your business. Using a **source and application of funds statement** will show you where financial resources have come from and where those funds have been utilised. It provides a link between your balance sheet and your profit and loss account to explain the difference between the financial resources of the business at the start and the end of the accounting period.

Additionally it is, of course, also possible for historic or projected figures to be used. Both historic and projected versions would be compiled in exactly the same way, using the same sources for the figure information. Provided you are consistent with the format that you use, it really does not matter how you choose to present the information.

At this stage it is important to remind you that you must retain adequate control over your debtors and creditors to ensure that cash is available as and when required to fund your business. Allowing your debtors too long to pay you could mean that you run out of cash and your creditors may not allow you to delay payment to them purely because of your lack of control over your finances.

Completing a source and application of funds statement will allow you to analyse and reconcile your financial performance. It will also give you an indication of how much reliance you are placing on the forbearance of your creditors, which under no circumstances should ever be abused. The statement can also be used in conjunction with **ratio analysis**, which is explained in the next section. This will ensure that your financial performance is consistent or improving, or allow you to take steps to rectify the position if it is deteriorating. For further information on how to compile a source and application of funds statement look at the Further Reading section.

USING RATIO ANALYSIS

A ratio is a means of comparing one figure with another to create a relationship between the figures which, when viewed in isolation, may have little meaning. A ratio is always made up of two parts, a numerator and a denominator, although both of these may involve a combination of figures.

There are also different ways to calculate some ratios. As with all forms of analysis it sometimes does not matter how you calculate the ratio. The important part is that you remain consistent and use the same comparable figures in exactly the same way. An example of such differences in calculation is given in the later section covering liquidity ratios with the example of stock turnover.

There are two key uses for ratio analysis:

- To provide a comparison between two or more variables in your accounts, either as a ratio of one to the other, or expressed as a percentage, or one as a multiple of the other.

- To compare the results from two or more sets of financial

accounts to disclose the trends and relationships between the figures that would not be evident from the figures alone.

Efficiency ratios

Efficiency ratios concentrate on your use of funds within the business. They look at the working capital elements within your accounts, e.g. stock, debtors and creditors, and establish just how good you are at controlling your finances. There are many different ways that each ratio can be calculated. For example, the sales to stock ratio can be expressed in at least three ways:

$$\frac{\text{Stock}}{\text{Sales}} = \text{Stock turnover ratio}$$

$$\frac{\text{Sales}}{\text{Stock}} = \text{Number of times stock turned over}$$

$$\frac{\text{Stock} \times 365}{\text{Sales}} = \text{Number of days sales of stock being held}$$

There are other inherent problems because the components are not valued in the same way. The sales figure is the actual selling price of the stock, but the stock contained in the balance sheet is valued at the lower of either cost or net realisable value. Additionally the stock figure could be inflated or deflated because it only relates to the holding on one day of the year.

In the case of stocks, the most common method is the final example above. This reveals approximately the number of days' stock that is being held which can vary quite widely depending on your business. If, for example, you sell fresh fruit and vegetables your stock holding would probably be no more than a few days. On the other hand, if you run a bookshop you may find that stock turnover, expressed in days, would be substantially longer.

As with all ratios the important aspect is the trend. An increase in the number of days could indicate that you are holding obsolete or damaged items that are ultimately unsaleable. The ideal position is that you only hold that amount of stock considered necessary at any one time.

Debtors and creditors

The other components of working capital, debtors and creditors, are calculated in the same way as stocks:

$$\frac{\text{Debtors} \times 365}{\text{Sales}} = \text{Time in days it takes you to collect payment from debtors}$$

Ideally the number of days should equate as closely as possible to your terms of trade. The faster you obtain payment the better because this will have a positive impact upon cash flow. If, however, the trend is showing an increase in the number of days this will require investigation for it could be due to some, or all, of the following:

- inadequate control over invoicing
- slow payment by debtors who are not being chased for payment
- potential bad debts
- market competition forcing an increase in your terms of trade.

Creditors are calculated in the same way using the formula:

$$\frac{\text{Creditors} \times 365}{\text{Sales}} = \text{Time in days that it takes you to pay your creditors}$$

This ratio will indicate how good you are at paying your creditors on time. It should also be compared to the terms of trade that you have with your suppliers. Any lengthening in the trend, whilst having a positive impact on cash flow, could also indicate problems. It may be that you are having to delay payment to your creditors for exactly that reason, a shortage of cash. This should be investigated, because if you are abusing your credit you could find the facility totally withdrawn with the subsequent severe impact on your finances.

Liquidity ratios
Liquidity ratios examine the relationship between assets and liabilities. They examine the cycle of funds through the business to ensure that stocks and debtors are turned into cash in order to pay creditors. The first ratio used for this purpose is the **current ratio**. This is calculated by dividing current assets and current liabilities as follows:

$$\frac{\text{Current assets}}{\text{Current liabilities}}$$

For a healthy business the resultant answer should be at least two. This would indicate that you have twice as many current assets than current liabilities and therefore should be able to meet your debts as they fall due. However, this ratio may distort the true liquid position because it assumes that stocks can be readily converted into cash. This may not be true in practice and therefore a liquidity ratio that excludes stock is also used. Known as the **acid test ratio** this is calculated as follows:

$$\frac{\text{Cash } + \text{ debtors}}{\text{Current liabilities}}$$

The resultant ratio in this case should not be less than one. Anything less would indicate that you could have liquidity problems and be unable to meet your debts as they fall due. It could also indicate that profit margins are being reduced or even that losses are being incurred.

Out of all the financial ratios, this one could be the most important to you in terms of control. Remember, cash is king. Run out of cash and your business could fail.

The final liquidity ratio calculates the relationship between the funds within the business that have been borrowed from outside sources as opposed to the funds that are invested from internal sources. In simple terms, this is the debt to equity ratio often referred to as the **gearing ratio** which was discussed in Chapter 1.

There is often argument about the exact external liabilities to be included in this ratio. Once again, this does not really matter provided you are consistent. It is better to look at the worst case scenario and include all sources of outside borrowing regardless of the term. The equity, or net worth of the business, includes the capital account and retained profits. It is sometimes referred to in the balance sheet as **surplus resources**. The gearing ratio is therefore calculated as follows:

$$\frac{\text{Total borrowing}}{\text{Net worth}}$$

Profitability ratios

As the name would suggest **profitability ratios** examine the trend in your profit margins. Profits can be shown in a variety of different stages within your profit and loss account although there are two that are commonly used, **gross profit** and **net profit**. In all cases the ratio is calculated as a percentage as follows:

$$\frac{\text{Profits} \times 100}{\text{Sales}}$$

The gross profit ratio will vary depending on what sort of business you operate. A manufacturing business could have a high cost overhead, which will mean a higher gross profit margin than perhaps a retailer with a high volume of sales but at a very fine margin.

Any declining trend in the gross profit ratio should be investigated because it indicates one or more of the following:

- Margins could be reducing due to competition in the market.

- The reduction could be due to increased purchase cost of the goods being sold which cannot be passed on to customers.

- The pricing strategy could be inadequate.

The net profit ratio represents the funds that are being retained in the business to finance future investment and growth. Variations in this ratio are caused by variations in the gross profit margin and the level of overhead expenses. It should show a steady or increasing trend. In the case of a declining trend in the net profit ratio which is not matched by a similar decline in the gross profit ratio this will indicate an increasing trend in overhead expenses. This will require investigation to establish the source of the increased expenditure to enable immediate corrective action.

KEY POINTS

- Make sure that you keep your market research up-to-date and retain your competitive advantage.

- Keep tight control over your finances – compare your actual performance against your forecasts and update your business plan accordingly.

- Understand the difference between cash and profit – run out of cash and your business will fail.

- Use ratio analysis to help improve your business but take care that you interpret the information correctly.

11

Dealing with Difficulties

At some stage of running your business you are going to encounter problems. The level of impact that they have on your business will depend to a large degree on what contingency plans you have in place to deal with them. Problems will not just be financial, they could be non-financial as well but have just as devastating an effect as financial problems. In this final chapter we will look at some of the problems that could occur and what sort of strategies you can have in place to deal with them.

FORMULATING CONTINGENCY PLANS

Problems can be minimised before a crisis occurs, mainly through forward planning. You will need to devise and implement everyday business procedures to minimise the chances of a crisis occurring in the first place. You will also want to work out what you should do if any particular crisis does occur.

The important part of planning is to take time to identify the possible crises that may affect your business. Think through why they might occur and how you can prevent them from happening. Consider how they would affect you and what has to be done to put things right if they happen despite your precautions. It is much easier to think through all the possibilities if you can involve other people.

Being prepared for a crisis

Crises can be classified into two main groups: external and internal.

- External crises are those which are outside the control of the business but which affect the business environment. They may include family problems or a bankrupt client leaving bad debts and order cancellations. More extreme examples of external crises are often classed as disasters, eg fire, flood, bomb alert or explosion.

- Internal crises are those which occur within the business. They often have little or no effect on the external environment. Examples include power or machinery failure, a computer crash, data corruption or something as simple as losing your diary.

It is absolutely essential that you have some form of crisis management plan which can be put into action as soon as a crisis occurs. In the next section we will look at the specific problems of dealing with problem debtors, the most common financial crisis likely to affect you. For the moment we need to concentrate on some of the ways that you can mitigate the non-financial problems that could occur.

A crisis of any degree can have an adverse affect on a business, ranging from disruptive to devastating, depending upon the severity of the problem and how prepared the business is to cope. If not properly managed, a crisis can lead to loss of earnings, reduction in profits and, ultimately, it may cause the business to go bankrupt. The damage caused by a crisis can, however, be minimised.

All possible remedial actions, for example the procedures and personal areas of responsibility of key employees, should be considered to work out the best course of action in any given crisis. There are four key areas that you will need to consider:

- Identification of the potential crisis.
- Gathering all possible information about the crisis and the circumstances which may lead up to it.
- Isolating the crisis.
- What action can be taken to resolve the crisis and any damage caused by it.

A draft contingency plan can then be drawn up and tested. Once this has been carried out the plans should be documented in a form that is easily accessible by all relevant staff. The contingency plan should be regularly revised, particularly after a crisis, so that it can be improved through the lessons that have been learnt.

Dealing with problem debtors

It is absolutely essential that you have a system in place to deal with all aspects of your debtor book. Initially, before you even grant any form of credit to a debtor, you will need to undertake some investigation as to whether they are actually creditworthy. You need to be entirely sure that when you grant credit to someone you know that they will have the means to pay you.

Never be afraid of refusing credit if you are in any doubt. You may lose the sale but it is better to lose the profit element on this sale than the whole amount of the sale itself by way of bad debt. Remember, you have not completed the sale until you are actually paid. All you have done is taken a gamble – consider the odds carefully before you place your bet.

It is crucial that you have some formal procedures in place to monitor your debtors. Some of these include:

- The imposition of a credit limit for each customer which you should never allow them to exceed.

- The monitoring of regular payments to clear the debt – as soon as payment becomes due make sure that it you chase it up.

- Once a payment becomes overdue do not allow further credit on the account – even if the credit limit has yet to be reached.

- If the debt becomes excessively overdue, for example your credit terms are 30 days and the debt has now been outstanding 60 days, then write to the customer demanding immediate payment.

- Follow up your letter after seven days with a further demand and giving notice that if necessary you will take legal action.

- If payment has still not been received after a further seven days then you should immediately consider issuing a summons. For debts of up to £5,000 these can be easily issued through a County Court.

At all costs do not be fobbed off with excuses for non-payment. You must remember that even small bad debts can have a devastating impact on your profit margins. Never, under any circumstances, allow any one customer an excessive amount of credit. A number of small businesses fail each year because of bad debts that they incur through dealing with apparently large, stable companies that go to the wall.

Insuring against problems

In Chapter 4 we looked at the types of personal insurance that you should consider when running your own business. You also need to consider adequate insurance for your business. You will need to seek specialist advice on exactly what type of insurance is relevant to your specific business. Examples of the type of insurance that may be applicable include:

- employers' liability insurance
- fire and other perils insurance
- theft insurance
- consequential loss insurance
- professional indemnity insurance
- keyman insurance.

Employers' liability insurance
If you employ anyone you must, by law, have employers' liability insurance. A copy of the relevant certificate of insurance must also be prominently displayed at all places of work.

Fire and other perils insurance
It is essential that you have adequate insurance to cover the possible destruction of your buildings through fire. You should also ensure that cover is in place for other perils, for example storm damage, flooding or explosions.

Theft insurance
This type of insurance will only normally cover thefts where a forced entry has been made. It does not usually cover such events as thefts by employees. If you do wish to insure against this you will need to arrange additional cover.

Consequential loss insurance
If your business does suffer a major catastrophe, which effectively stops you trading for a time, this type of cover will insure against the loss of profits. It may also cover your employee costs and the costs of establishing interim trading premises.

Professional indemnity insurance
If you are in a service-based business offering expert advice, as I am as a consultant, it is essential that you have adequate professional indemnity insurance to cover you against claims by your clients for damages caused by your negligence. In some cases it will be required in any event as a condition of your membership of a professional body.

Keyman insurance
If you have one or more key members of staff on whom the business depends for success you should consider keyman insurance. This will pay out a lump sum in the event of that person's death to enable you to keep the business going whilst you find a suitable successor.

AVOIDING DISASTER

It is a clearly established statistic that businesses are more likely to fail in their first five years of trading. Whilst the chances of success increase the older and more experienced the business and indeed the management become, it can take up to ten years before the business is on a firm foundation.

One of the major causes of failure is inexperience in managing all aspects of running a business at the same time. For example, you may be a first class plumber but unless you manage your time and your work quotations in order to make a profit you will fail in business. Unfortunately many business owners are quick to blame others when the actual causes of failure are their own shortcomings. The bank manager features high on the list of causes being blamed for the business failure due to the lack of provision of additional finance.

Reasons for failure
To expand upon this a little further, in surveys conducted amongst small businesses the common reasons for failure were cited as:

- further funding being turned down
- lack of sales
- late payment by debtors – cash flow problems
- increased competition from larger firms.

Professional advisors, however, have a totally different view on the major causes of failure – they place the blame squarely on poor management. The reasons that they give include:

- lack of capital
- targets are not set and properly reviewed
- performance, especially financial, is not monitored
- corrective action, if any, is taken far too late
- market research is not kept up to date
- turnover is chased instead of profit.

The last of these, often referred to as 'overtrading', is not recognised at all by some businesses. They consider that they must increase turnover as quickly as possible although they lack the working capital to support the expansion. You can fail through achieving too many sales just as quickly as you can through having too few sales.

Having a clear way forward

There are a number of things that you can do to help you succeed. It is an established fact that businesses that seek professional advice and training on running their business tend to have a greater survival rate. You can see from the list of reasons above, given by professional advisors, the sort of planning that you should be doing. In simple terms, once you have established your business you need to:

- Update your original business plan on a regular basis.

- Constantly monitor your financial performance to enable early corrective action to be taken.

- Concentrate on making a profit and not just the volume of sales.

- Take advantage of as much training in all aspects of running a business as you can – in most cases it is offered free of charge or at a very small cost.

- Keep looking at conditions in the market – do not be caught out by the actions of competitors which could remove your competitive advantage.

TALKING TO THE FUNDER

The threat of business failure will be an extremely traumatic event. You cannot afford to stick your head in the sand and hope that problems will go away. It is up to you to try to stop the business failing and you need all the help you can get. It is absolutely essential that you talk to any funders to whom you owe money. Unless they are prepared to support you and help you try to get back on track you will undoubtedly fail.

The important point to remember is that if a funder has invested in your business it is also in their own interests to try to turn the position around. What you must not do is to carry on issuing cheques drawn on your bank account unless you have sufficient funds, or are within an agreed overdraft facility, to pay them.

Controlling your own account

Let me make it clear from the outset that once you lose control of your bank account you have lost control of your business. It is no longer you who is deciding what should be paid out, it is your bank manager. You must keep tight control over all the components of working capital and that includes your bank account.

If you have been granted an overdraft facility it is essential that you do not exceed the overdraft limit without the bank's permission. Quite apart from the penalty interest that will be imposed, in some cases equating to over 30% per annum, the bank may refuse to pay cheques or other items such as direct debits. If this happens you can expect to incur further bank charges of around £30 for every item that is returned.

More importantly, you will have lost the confidence of your bank manager. If you had been to see them and talked through the problem, they may have been able to help you find a solution. It would, of course, have been even better if you had seen the problem coming before it actually occurred which would have given you time to do something about it.

Talking through your plans

Let us assume that disaster is not looming as aforesaid and that you have taken all the necessary steps to monitor your business. On updating your cash flow projections you discover that the business is doing quite well but you will need additional finance in the next few months. Now is the time to take action. You have given yourself the chance to make fresh plans. More importantly, you have given yourself options.

The first thing to do is to think through what options you have. With a likely deficit in cash flow there are two basic options. You can either defer some of the expenditure, if it is not necessary, or you can seek additional cash. This will take you right back to the first chapter in this book. You need to put together fresh proposals.

Once you have done that you can start the whole process of business planning and fund-raising again. Once your new proposals have been put together you can then talk them through with your funders. If your original proposals have been successful you will stand a good chance of gaining additional support. The important aspect is communication. Always keep in regular contact with your funders and, more importantly, do not be afraid to talk through your future plans. They want to see you succeed and should, therefore, do anything that they can to assist you.

Asking for help

Contrary to the previous section, let us now assume that business failure seems inevitable. You now need expert help and fast. You will need to minimise the financial loss involved and realise as many of your business assets as you can. At this stage you also need to be aware that even if you are trading as a limited liability company, under some circumstances, especially where you continue to trade despite the fact that your business is insolvent, the protection of limited liability is lost. You may become personally liable for the debts of your business and face a criminal investigation.

It is absolutely essential that you face your problems and seek expert professional help. In the first instance it is probably worth approaching your business support organisation for help, but if the position is too bad they may not wish to be involved. They will, however, point you in the right direction, probably into the arms of a licensed insolvency practitioner.

If this does happen you must co-operate fully because they are the experts in the field of winding up a business and, apart from working to gain as much as possible for your creditors, they will also be working in your best interests. Hopefully, however, you will have heeded all the other advice in this book and this final section will never be applicable to you.

KEY POINTS

- Sooner or later you will face a problem of one form or another – if you are prepared to deal with it, it should never result in a major crisis.

- Do not allow your debtors to take advantage of you – you need them to pay you on time in order to pay your own creditors.

- Make sure that all your insurance is adequate – this is not an area in which it is advisable to try to cut costs.

- Understand the key causes of business failure and make sure that they will never apply to you.

- Business planning and monitoring is an ongoing process – it does not stop when you raise the funds that you require.

- If you do recognise that problems are on the way, financial or otherwise, seek help at the earliest possible opportunity.

Appendix
Sample Business Plan Template

SECTION ONE – CONTACT DETAILS

This should be no more than a single page and contain clear details of the company or trading name, the registered and trading address and contact name with telephone and fax numbers together with e-mail and website address if appropriate.

It should also contain details of any advisors that may have assisted you in the formulation of the Business Plan such as an Accountant or Solicitor.

SECTION TWO – SYNOPSIS

A short synopsis of the Business Plan should be given – usually no more than a few paragraphs – but to ensure that the reader is aware from the outset exactly what the Plan is all about, what it has been written for, and what is being sought – if seeking funding, which is more often than not the reason for Business Plans, state exactly how much, for what, and how long it will take to repay.

This section should be written after all the other components of the Business Plan have been put together.

SECTION THREE – BUSINESS BACKGROUND AND HISTORY

Quite obviously if the reader has no real knowledge of the business there is a need to make sure that a full background and history is provided covering when the business was started, how it has developed since then, any significant mile-stones or achievements, any accreditation gained such as quality standard awards or awards from Industrial or other bodies.

This is the place to really sell the business to the reader in order that they can establish exactly what has been achieved since commencing trading.

If, as in the case of a new business, there is no background history then it needs to include details of why the business is starting up and short details of the owner's own background and experience.

Do not include too much information on this final aspect as this will be covered in a later section but make sure to include details of any special skills, or research that has been undertaken which has led the founders of the business to consider starting up.

SECTION FOUR – THE PRODUCT

Give a precise description of exactly what it is that the business will be doing with specific details of any range of products or services.

It is also important that it is outlined quite clearly what the products or services will do for the consumer, and what differentiates this product or service from those that may already be available in the market.

In other words outline the competitive advantages that the business will offer over and above the competition.

SECTION FIVE – OPERATIONAL PROCESS

This section is only really appropriate to any firm that is involved in direct manufacturing of a product.

If this is appropriate then full details of the exact procedures required from the basic ordering of raw materials right through all of the production stages to achieve the final finished product should be given.

Please however bear in mind that the target audience may not be able to understand any jargon that is used so do make sure that whilst it is explained exactly how the finished product is achieved, keep it simple.

If necessary, if the process is long and complicated involving numerous production stages, then merely use a flow diagram and bullet points.

SECTION SIX – MARKET ANALYSIS

For any business this is one of the most important sections of the Business Plan because it deals with the overall market and should establish exactly how the business specifically operates in that market. Specific details should therefore be given with as much information as possible in terms of:

- The overall size of the market, both domestic and international.

- Trends within that market – supported by relevant figures.

- Specific details of direct competitors – who they are, what they do and how they compare.

- Market segmentation in terms of trade, retail, wholesale and mail order.

- Pricing expectations.

- Potential customers.

- Quality and service standards.

- Relevant legislation such as Health and Safety.

- Environmental concerns.

- Relevant independent market research information if available.

This can never be an exhaustive list and each Business Plan will require differing Market Analysis depending on the market in which the business operates.

SECTION SEVEN – MARKETING STRATEGY

Using the information gained from the Market Analysis the business can now start to formulate the Marketing Strategy and the initial stage will probably involve the use of a SWOT analysis.

This will set out in a logical manner the Strengths, Weaknesses, Opportunities and Threats and whilst this may not be used in the actual analysis within the Business Plan it will assist in formulating the Marketing Strategy around the five key components.

- Customers and markets – A clear understanding of the potential customers and markets needs to be shown. In other words whom are you going to sell your products or services to?

- Product – what it is that the business will sell, remember this has been covered previously and therefore only a brief description is necessary with comparisons to any existing products gleaned from the analysis.

- Price – how much will be charged and how this figure has been calculated. How does it compare to the competition and what sort of margin or mark-up has been used and why.

- Promotion – how will the business advertise it's product or service and where. How much will it cost and over what period i.e. will there be a large product launch campaign followed by smaller adverts in the following time periods.

- Place – where will the business operate from and why. How will the products be distributed and where will they be sold through.

It is vitally important that the business achieves what is known as the correct 'Marketing Mix' within the strategy with all components correctly balanced.

As an example there is little point in trying to sell the product on a pure price basis when the market research that you carried out for the Market Analysis tells you that customers are looking for a high quality product.

SECTION EIGHT – THE PROJECT

This section should give a short synopsis of the project which will in effect summarise the next few sections.

Details should be given of the reasons behind the project, exactly what it is and what benefits it will bring to the business such as cost savings in addition to which summarised details of job creation and capital expenditure should be outlined.

Most importantly of all set out the finance required and exactly what that funding will be used for i.e. working capital in terms of revenue expenditure or fixed capital for expenditure on assets such as premises and equipment.

As with section two, this section is best left until all other parts of the Business Plan have been put together.

SECTION NINE – MANAGEMENT STRUCTURE

Where there are only a limited number of key personnel, as in the case of sole traders or small partnerships, a full background profile should be inserted here for every member of the management team. For larger organisations it is necessary to show a full management structure diagram clearly showing levels of responsibility and reporting lines.

In all cases full details of all members of the management team should be given which clearly show the experience and skills that they bring to the business, and in the case of any anticipated new members of the team, exactly what skills will be necessary to do the job and whether in fact there is anyone in mind to fill the position.

SECTION TEN – HUMAN RESOURCES

Full details should be set out here in table format of all staff presently employed together with projections for the required levels of staff over the next three years.

Where additional staff are required for the expansion of the business then details should be given of specific responsibilities and potential salary or wage and if possible, if the new members of staff are required in the short term, what efforts have been made to recruit or indeed if there is already a potential candidate.

SECTION ELEVEN – PREMISES AND EQUIPMENT

For existing businesses give exact details of the present trading premises in terms of freehold or leasehold or rented with details of monthly or annual rental payments, length of lease, review dates and possible market valuation.

For new businesses give details of proposed location and as above whether freehold, leasehold or rented, rental payments, proposed length of lease and likely start date. Details of capital expenditure should also be given in table format for all equipment to be purchased over the life of the Business Plan, usually three years.

If relevant, reasons for such purchases should be given especially where such new equipment will bring about cost savings or greater operational efficiency.

SECTION TWELVE – FINANCIAL INFORMATION

Summarised tables should be provided of the business's previous financial statements and of the forecasted Cash Flow, Profit and Loss and Balance sheets in order that comparisons can be seen in a simple logical format.

It is also useful to provide summarised accounting ratios for comparison purposes. For example gross and net profit, gearing and liquidity.

If the business is involved in Importing or Exporting, full details in terms of percentage sales and purchases should be given.

In the case of separate groups of products or services these should be split as far as possible with specific details of percentage sales and related direct costs.

SECTION THIRTEEN – FUNDING REQUIREMENT

If appropriate set out details of existing finance available such as Bank overdrafts and specific details of the new finance being sought in terms of type of funding, i.e. Bank Loan or increased overdraft, Hire Purchase, Leasing, Equity via either Venture Capital or Business Angel.

Also set out the existing capital structure of the business in terms of issued share capital or owner's capital and whether this is to be changed.

In the case of a new start business details should also be given of the opening capital to be injected, and if relevant the source of that injection whether it be in terms of cash or introduction of assets.

Finally set out the timing and source of repayment, usually in terms of retained profits as evidenced by the Profit and Loss forecasts, or less frequently, in the case of equity capital provided by Venture Capitalists the anticipated stock flotation time-table.

SECTION FOURTEEN – RISK EVALUATION

The final section of the Business Plan is devoted to a sensitivity analysis looking at what may happen in the event of variations in the Business Plan forecasts and what could be done to minimise the risk both to the business and the potential funders.

This must clearly demonstrate that all possible risks have been considered, such as a downturn in overall turnover or a reduced overall profit margin due to perhaps increased costs and that within the Business Plan you have allowed for such risks with contingency strategies.

Useful Contacts

British Chambers of Commerce, Manning House, 22 Carlisle Place, London SW1P 1JA. Tel: (020) 7565 2000. Fax: (020) 7565 2049. www.britishchambers.org.uk

British Trade International, Department of Trade and Industry, Kingsgate House, 66–74 Victoria Street, London SW1E 6SW. www.dti.gov.uk

British Venture Capital Association, Essex House, 12–13 Essex Street, London WC2R 3AA. Tel: (020) 7240 3846. www.bvca.co.uk

Business Link Signpost Line. Tel: (0345) 567765. www.businesslink.co.uk

Department of Trade and Industry. www.dti.gov.uk

EUREKA. www.eureka.be

European Structural Funds. www.dti.gov.uk/europe/structural.html

Federation of Small Businesses, Whittle Way, Blackpool Business Park, Blackpool, Lancashire FY24 2FE. Tel: (01253) 336000. www.fsb.org.uk

The Forum of Private Business, Ruskin Chambers, Drury Lane, Knutsford, Cheshire WA16 6HA. Tel: (01565) 634467. www.fpb.co.uk

Link Directorate, Office of Science and Technology, Department of Trade and Industry, UG88, 1 Victoria Street, London SW1H 0ET. Tel: (020) 7215 0053. Fax: (020) 7215 0054. www.dti.gov.uk/ost/link

National Business Angels Network, 40–42 Cannon Street, London EC4N 6JJ. Tel: (020) 7329 4141. www.nationalbusangels.co.uk

National Federation of Enterprise Agencies, Trinity Gardens, 9–11 Bromham Road, Bedford MK40 2UQ. Tel: (01234) 354 055.

The Phoenix Fund, Small Business Service, Social Inclusion Unit, St Mary's House, Moorfoot, Sheffield S1 4PQ. www.businessadviceonline.org/press/phoenix.asp

Shell *Live*WIRE, Hawthorn House, Forth Banks, Newcastle-upon-Tyne NE1 3SG. Tel: (0345) 573252. www.shell-livewire.org

Small Business Service. www.businessadviceonline.org

Small Firms Loan Guarantee Scheme. www.businessadviceonline.org/SFLGS/

Small Firms Merit Award for Research and Technology (SMART) www.businessadviceonline.org/SMART

Trade Partners UK. www.tradepartners.gov.uk

Phil Stone, Author and Management Consultant, Parkstone Management Consultancy, 9 Parkstone Close, Hastings Hill, Sunderland, Tyne and Wear SR4 9PA. E-mail: help@pkstone.demon.co.uk Website: http://www.pkstone.demon.co.uk (Links to all of the websites above together with a large number of other useful sites can be obtained direct from this site.)

Further Reading

Make Marketing Work For You, Phil Stone (How To Books).
The Ultimate Business Plan, Phil Stone (How To Books).
Understanding Financial Accounts, Phil Stone (How To Books).